Praise for
Negotiating Peace and Confronting Corruption

"This book effectively analyzes the characteristics and effects of building anti-corruption provisions into negotiated settlements in post civil war situations."
—**Jens Andvig,** research professor, department of international economics, Norwegian Institute of International Affairs

"The enduring prevalence of corruption in conflict-affected countries is frequently bemoaned but rarely addressed in ways that lead to its reduction. Bert Spector's Negotiating Peace and Confronting Corruption *fills this gap with a cogent analysis that connects symptoms to causes of corruption and recommends paying attention to corruption as an integral component of negotiating peace and mitigating conflict. Through a comparative analysis of six cases, the author illustrates lessons learned for reducing corruption and improving governance and provides practical advice on how to incorporate anticorruption measures into peace accords and improve the prospects for successful implementation."*
—**Derick W. Brinkerhoff,** Distinguished Fellow in International Public Management, RTI International

"Most contemporary anticorruption strategies employ the language and symbolism of struggle, and emphasize law enforcement and punishment. Yet many of the worst corruption problems arise in postconflict societies, where institutions are weak and trust is fragile—at best. In those settings confrontational reforms are unlikely to be credible and may well make matters worse for citizens who have suffered much already. In this book, Bertram Spector lays out constructive and useful anticorruption alternatives based on careful analyses of tough cases. Negotiation can build trust and encourage the development of incentives and consensual standards that can not only check the abuse of power but also contribute to peacebuilding and reconstruction. Reformers in many places will look at their challenges differently, and in more constructive ways, once they have considered the lessons Spector develops in these pages."
—**Michael Johnston,** Colgate University

"This volume is a very important piece of work that demonstrates that anticorruption measures need to be introduced early enough alongside other provisions for good governance to achieve results."
—**Diana Klein,** International Alert

"Bert Spector has written an extremely useful study, conceptually focused and framed in its analysis, and most pertinent for bringing conflicted states back into responsible governance. His cases studies are concise and comprehensive, and his conclusions are sharp and insightful for practitioners and analysts. A most excellent and unusual treatment of corruption and, better yet, how to handle it."

—**I. William Zartman,** Jacob Blaustein Professor Emeritus of International Organization and Conflict Resolution, Johns Hopkins University, School of Advanced International Studies

Negotiating Peace and Confronting Corruption

NEGOTIATING PEACE AND CONFRONTING CORRUPTION

Challenges for Postconflict Societies

Bertram I. Spector

UNITED STATES INSTITUTE OF PEACE
WASHINGTON, D.C.

The views expressed in this book are those of the author alone. They do not necessarily reflect the views of the United States Institute of Peace.

United States Institute of Peace
2301 Constitution Ave., NW
Washington, DC 20037
www.usip.org

First published 2011

To request permission to photocopy or reprint materials for course use, contact the Copyright Clearance Center at www.copyright.com. For print, electronic media, and all other subsidiary rights, e-mail permissions@usip.org.

Printed in the United States of America

The paper used in this publication meets the minimum requirements of American National Standards for Information Science—Permanence of Paper for Printed Library Materials, ANSI Z39.48-1984.

Library of Congress Cataloging-in-Publication Data

Spector, Bertram I. (Bertram Irwin), 1949-
Negotiating peace and confronting corruption : challenges for post-conflict societies / Bertram I. Spector.
p. cm.
Includes bibliographical references.
ISBN 978-1-60127-071-9 (pbk. : alk. paper)
1. Diplomatic negotiations in international disputes. 2. Peace-building. 3. Post-war reconstruction. 4. Corruption—Prevention. I. Title.
JV6045.S64 2011
303.6'9—dc22
2010052950

For my mother, Rose Teicher,
who instilled in me values of integrity
and a love of the written word

Contents

Acknowledgments

This book brings together my longtime research interests in three separate fields—international negotiation, anticorruption, and development assistance. At the nexus of these interests lies the welfare of postconflict countries undergoing sensitive peacebuilding programs. The balancing of effective negotiations that address grievances concerning government corruption with the implementation of closely aligned and targeted donor assistance is a developing art. The ultimate peace, security, effectiveness, and integrity of fragile states emerging from violent conflict rest on how well these three processes are carried out and integrated.

I acknowledge, with great appreciation, the support provided by the United States Institute of Peace and the Jacob and Hilda Blaustein Foundation through grants to the Center for Negotiation Analysis to examine the confluence of these critical processes. I am also grateful to the United States Agency for International Development and Management Systems International for providing opportunities to study the development assistance aspects of confronting corruption in postconflict settings.

The author recognizes the enthusiastic efforts of Ketevan Nozadze and Tara Thwing, who supported the collection and analysis of the case data on anticorruption international development assistance. Thanks also go to Elizabeth Hart, Svetlana Winbourne, and Michael Lund for their insightful comments on early sections of the research and to several anonymous reviewers of the manuscript who offered excellent recommendations to improve the manuscript. I am extremely grateful to Michelle Slavin and Brian Slattery, who managed the review and editing process quickly and skillfully. Lastly, thanks to my wife, Judy, for her support and advice during the development of this book.

The opinions, findings, and conclusions or recommendations expressed in this report are those of the author and do not necessarily reflect the views of the United States Institute of Peace, the Blaustein Foundation, or the United States Agency for International Development.

1

Emerging from Corruption
and Conflict

A member of the Iraqi national assembly was indicted for embez-
zling millions of foreign assistance dollars that had been meant to
protect a key oil pipeline. He used those funds to support insurgents
who attacked the very same pipeline.[1] In a separate incident, the former Iraqi
defense minister was also charged with corruption for misspending $1.3 bil-
lion in military contracts. Kickbacks, bribery, speed money, nepotism, and
other forms of corruption are currently widespread in Iraq. Similar episodes
have been recounted in postconflict Bosnia and Mozambique.[2] A culture of
corruption in countries emerging from violent conflict—usually nurtured
during a period of reconstruction and rapid ramp-up of foreign assistance,
and in the context of ineffective institutions and very limited rule of law to
control such indiscretions—depletes the public coffers, limits the delivery of
quality public services, reduces public trust in government, scares off investors, and reduces the prospects for economic growth.

Problems of widespread corruption are even more acute in postconflict
contexts than in ordinary development situations. Corruption, defined as the
abuse of entrusted authority for private gain, is sometimes characterized as a
problem of wealth seeking power or power seeking wealth.[3] But in countries
emerging from conflict, corruption may be catalyzed by ideological as well as

---

1. Robert Worth and James Glanz, "Oil Graft Fuels the Insurgency, Iraq and U.S. Say," *New York Times*, February 5, 2006.

2. For Bosnia, see Vera Devine, "Corruption in Post-War Reconstruction: The Experience of Bosnia and Herzegovina," May 25, 2003, http://www.tiri.org/images/stories/NIR%20Documents/PWR%20Bosnia&Herz%20Devine.pdf (accessed November 2010). For Mozambique, see Joseph Hanlon, "Do Donors Promote Corruption? The Case of Mozambique," *Third World Quarterly* 25, no. 4 (2004), 747–763.

3. Samuel Huntington, *Political Order in Changing Societies* (New Haven, CT: Yale University Press, 1968).

baser greed-seeking motives. Even after a peace agreement is signed, losing factions with unresolved grievances may still seek power to promote their cause, funding their efforts through corrupt means.[4] The chaos in the aftermath of violent conflict can reverse peace gains if corruption weakens already inefficient governance structures, reducing the hopes for economic growth and increasing the power of spoilers, who can cause backsliding toward renewed instability and conflict.[5] But corruption certainly is not reserved for spoilers; those who assume power after conflict may take advantage of their positions to raid state coffers and exploit donor assistance with impunity, enriching themselves at the expense of the public. And charges of corruption against one's enemies are a frequently abused weapon among rivals.

To have the intended effect and persist over the long term, peace negotiations need to help parties address the factors that created the conflict in the first place. Experience demonstrates that effective anticorruption practices and institutions can give postconflict countries greater opportunities for a stable peace and positive economic and social development. Donor organizations can stimulate appropriate anticorruption mechanisms through special funding and technical assistance in the postconflict period. In some cases, anticorruption initiatives have been embedded in negotiated peace agreements.

After years of conflict, the path to peace typically is complicated, and merely negotiating a cease-fire may not be enough to achieve a sustainable peace; ending violence by itself may not necessarily resolve the underlying causes of conflict. The roots of strife may be traced to grievances tied to racial or ethnic discrimination, violations of human or civil rights, or economic inequalities. Injustices may have emanated from bad governance practices and abuses of power, such as a lack of leadership commitment to the public good, inequalities and inequities, ineffectual use of office, misconduct, unaccountable decisions and nontransparent procedures, an absence of or disregard for the rule of law, and barriers to public participation in decision making. Corruption and the abuse of office may be a key factor.

Continued bad or weak governance—and the corruption that often accompanies it—can sabotage democratic and economic growth. On the

---

4. Karen Ballentine and Heiko Nitzschke, "Beyond Greed and Grievance: Policy Lessons from Studies in the Political Economy of Armed Conflict," International Peace Academy Policy Report, New York, 2003.

5. Stephen John Stedman, "Spoiler Problems in Peace Processes," in Paul C. Stern and Daniel Druckman, eds. *International Conflict Resolution after the Cold War* (Washington, DC: National Academies Press, 2000); and Marie-Joelle Zahar, "Reframing the Spoiler Debate in Peace Processes," in *Contemporary Peacemaking: Conflict, Violence, and Peace Processes* (New York: Palgrave Macmillan, 2003).

other hand, negotiating and embedding future good governance reforms and corruption controls into peace agreements can complement cease-fires with improved delivery of public services and more transparent, accountable, and predictable government, in accordance with the rule of law and democratic standards. Negotiating the repair and strengthening of essential government functions means that the peace process must look forward after conflict, seeking to address past grievances by fighting corruption and implementing good governance procedures.[6]

Good governance reforms and corruption controls that can be negotiated into peace agreements are what we call *integrity provisions*. These provisions seek to make right what was wrong in the way the society had been governed. They aspire to make public officials accountable for their actions, enforce the rule of law, make it more difficult for authorities to abuse the public, and ensure that government operates on a level playing field for all. Integrity provisions do this by inserting control mechanisms into governance processes, simplifying administrative transactions, making the detection and punishment for corrupt behavior more predictable, and ensuring transparency and openness in government decision making, for example.

However, designing improved integrity provisions and safeguards against corruption may not be enough to promote long-lasting peace and stability; these provisions need to be implemented in practice. The parties to the peace agreement, as well as interested bilateral donors and international organizations, must support the implementation of these provisions and safeguards through technical and financial assistance. The goal is not to impose Western ideals, but to support the fragile new state through the challenges and obstacles it will face during the first few years of peace, by building local capacity and ownership.

All the above elements together—a negotiated end to violence, agreement on good governance reforms and anticorruption controls in the peace accords, and provision of adequate and timely development assistance—establish the principles, frameworks, and formulas of good intentions. These need to be implemented through concrete, practical, and forthright measures. Especially within the difficult, unstable, and transitional circumstances of postconflict societies, this requires a high degree of political will, resources, and technical capacity that sometimes has to compete with new and old demands and interests of a multitude of stakeholders, some of whom were parties to the negotiated accords and some who were not.

---

6.   I. William Zartman and Victor Kremenyuk, eds., *Peace versus Justice: Negotiating Forward- and Backward-Looking Outcomes* (Lanham, MD: Rowman and Littlefield Publishers, 2005).

One more essential factor for planning stable and long-term peace is the establishment of a postagreement regime to provide a channel for all parties to negotiate practical details and renegotiate provisions, given the broad principles typically agreed to in the original peace negotiations.[7] Postagreement negotiation forums offer a way for stakeholders—preferably all stakeholders—to find new solutions to the new problems that develop in the course of implementing peace agreements. More nuanced governance mechanisms can often be devised and implemented after postconflict agreements have had a chance to either prove themselves or demonstrate their deficiencies. In continuing the dialogue, negotiation forums allow parties to voice their demands and improve on the original agreement.[8]

Thus, a stable long-term peace that can rebuild integrity into government appears to be the product of a four-stage process: cease-fire negotiations, negotiations over future governance regimes, implementation of the negotiated agreements with the support of development assistance, and continuing postagreement negotiation dialogue and public participation to improve on the original agreement.

Corruption and Governance

Legal definitions of corrupt behavior typically connect misuse of public office to personal greed. Poor governance, on the other hand, can involve the misuse of office due to ineptness, inefficiency, mismanagement, lack of resources, or apathy. Governance is a broad concept within which corruption is an important dimension, and problems of both corruption and governance are often situated at the nexus of grievances that initiate internal conflicts and need to be remedied in the peace process if they are to be resolved once and for all.

Authorities are seen to provide good governance if they are predictable, develop policy openly, operate professionally and for the public good, and function within the rule of law and with the participation of civil society. Poor governance is the opposite, characterized by arbitrary policymaking, unaccountable bureaucracies, unenforced and unjust legal systems, the abuse

7. Bertram Spector and I. William Zartman, *Getting It Done: International Regimes and Postagreement Negotiations* (Washington, DC: United States Institute of Peace Press, 2003).

8. Such postagreement negotiation processes can be considered a practical demonstration of Ghani and Lockhart's concept of internal compacts, by which domestic stakeholders and the state develop channels for continued dialogue in postconflict societies to find peaceful ways to avert further conflict, strengthen democratic systems, and build stable institutions. See Ashraf Ghani and Clare Lockhart, *Fixing Failed States* (New York: Oxford University Press 2008).

of executive power, and an unengaged civil society.[9] Corrupt behavior is inhibited by the former and facilitated by the latter. But to a large extent, the phenomena are closely correlated: The elements that allow poor governance to thrive also open the door to corrupt behavior.

Corruption, Conflict, and Negotiation

One of the oldest human practices, corruption is often a potent cause of conflict, catalyzing a wide range of grievances against government by various social groups. Corrupt practices can also thrive after conflict, when laws and institutions have not been fully reestablished with the authority, respect, transparency, and accountability needed to ward off potential abuse from public officials. Various forms of corruption—embezzlement, nepotism, bribery, extortion, influence peddling, and fraud, at petty or grand levels—can easily emerge where the rule of law is not firmly rooted and it appears that nobody is watching the store. Where impunity prevails, corruption is a low-risk, high-gain activity.

As mentioned above, corruption can be a major impediment to development and growth after conflict. It can hijack crucial state and donor funds intended for rebuilding infrastructure, providing basic services, and creating the framework for a renewed economy. It can also generate the foundations for a criminal state, facilitating drug trafficking, human trafficking, money laundering, piracy, and terrorism. Weak institutions paired with an influx of outside funds, typical in postconflict circumstances, contribute to the potential growth of corruption.[10] When corruption pervades elections, accountability is lost. When corruption infuses the judiciary, the rule of law is the victim. When corruption infiltrates the health and education sectors, the vulnerable and the youth suffer. Corruption undermines the legitimacy and effectiveness of government and reduces public trust. It also obstructs economic development, raising the cost of doing business, reducing fair competition, and increasing the risks of broken commercial contracts and agreements.

Even as the international community has elevated the problem of corruption on the public agenda in both the developed and developing world since the mid-1990s, the annual Transparency International scoring of countries

---

9. Organization for Economic Cooperation and Development (OECD), *Citizens as Partners: OECD Handbook on Information, Consultation and Public Participation in Policy-Making* (Paris: OECD, 2001); and World Bank, *Governance, The World Bank's Experience* (Washington, DC: World Bank, 1994).

10. Susan Rose-Ackerman, "Corruption and Post-Conflict Peace-Building," *Ohio Northern Law Review* 15, no. 3 (2008), 328–343.

shows pervasive corruption to be a major and continuing issue for both rich and poor nations. The special case of countries emerging from violent conflict and their inherent fragility makes susceptibility to corruption—and its negative implications of slowed economic and democratic growth—that much more critical and in need of urgent remedies.

Le Billon confirmed the link between corruption and conflict.[11] When good governance collapses during and after conflict, people often resort to corruption merely to get things done, and while this can have short-term positive effects, among its possible long-term consequences are renewed conflict by peace spoilers, reduced governance ability, continuing economic decline, and state capture by organized crime. In some cases, such corruption has been controlled, at least temporarily, under difficult postconflict settings, for example, in Mozambique initially under an idealistic Frente de Libertação de Moçambique (FRELIMO) leadership and in Afghanistan initially under the Taliban, despite those regimes' other excesses. But these seem to be the exceptions.

Bolongaita observed several interlocking vicious cycles among corruption, conflict, and poverty.[12] Most countries experiencing either conflict or postconflict situations rank very low on the World Bank governance indicator for corruption and very low on Transparency International's corruption perception index. Countries rated by the World Bank as heavily indebted poor countries also cluster together among the most highly corrupt countries on the World Bank's control of corruption index. Another study found that corruption only indirectly causes poverty, but that poverty provides the breeding grounds for systemic corruption.[13] In any case, it is fairly certain that lack of effective governance, high levels of conflict, and low economic growth are strong correlates of high levels of corruption. A seminal study by Mauro supported the idea that these factors are closely linked.[14] He found that an improvement in a country's corruption index from a score of six to eight on a ten-point scale increases the investment rate by more than 4 percent and annual per capita gross domestic product (GDP) growth by nearly

---

11. Philippe Le Billon, "Overcoming Corruption in the Wake of Conflict," in Transparency International, *Global Corruption Report* (London: Pluto Press, 2005).

12. Emil Bolongaita, "Controlling Corruption in Post-Conflict Countries," Occasional Paper no. 26, Joan B. Kroc Institute for International Peace Studies, University of Notre Dame, South Bend, IN, January 2005.

13. Eric Chetwynd, Frances Chetwynd and Bertram Spector, "Corruption and Poverty: A Review of Recent Literature," Washington, DC: Management Systems International, June 2003).

14. Paolo Mauro, "The Effects of Corruption on Growth and Public Expenditure," in Arnold J. Heidenheimer and Michael Johnston, eds., *Political Corruption: Concepts and Contexts,* 3rd ed. (New Brunswick, NJ: Transaction Publishers, 2002).

one-half of a percent. The potential benefits of reducing corruption appear to be concrete and substantial.

Bolongaita made three recommendations to control corruption in post-conflict countries: ensure that corruption is identified as a serious risk and a priority issue to be addressed; develop anticorruption measures early in the postconflict process or even during peace negotiations; and ensure that the commitment and resources are made available to implement anticorruption provisions effectively.[15] On a more tactical level, Le Billon recommended three major efforts to reduce corruption in postconflict reconstruction periods: ensure public support and demand to fight corruption, build the economic and regulatory context to reduce opportunities for corruption, and secure an adequate legal framework.[16] To these researchers, it is clear that reducing corruption should be a priority in postconflict reconstruction settings—and the earlier the better.

Zartman found that almost one-third of civil wars conclude in negotiation, despite the asymmetry between the conflicting parties, the dynamics of insurgencies, and painful stalemates.[17] An external mediator often is crucial to bringing the parties to the negotiating table. Governance issues may be treated explicitly in the negotiations—as in the 1999 Sierra Leone and the 2001 Papua New Guinea peace agreements—or implicitly, taking a backseat to generating the peace itself. If governance issues, in any form, can be addressed in the peace accords, they must be implemented effectively in the postagreement period. Spector and Zartman, in a U.S. Institute of Peace-sponsored project on postagreement negotiation, analyzed the importance of this stage and the role that continued negotiation can play in embedding negotiated provisions into governing practice.[18] When governance provisions are not negotiated explicitly in the peace accords, then development assistance programs in the postagreement period can help to foster anticorruption initiatives.

Peace negotiations can address past wrongs traced to corruption and future backsliding toward corrupt practices. Such negotiations provide the context for parties to talk about past injustices that brought on the conflict, while developing mechanisms to prevent their reoccurrence. Negotiations must present a vision of the future to all combatants who are parties in the hoped-for

---

15. Bolongaita, "Controlling Corruption."

16. Le Billon, "Overcoming Corruption."

17. I. William Zartman, ed., *Elusive Peace: Negotiating an End to Civil Wars* (Washington, DC: Brookings Institution Press, 1995).

18. Spector and Zartman, *Getting It Done.*

solution, offering a complex mix and balancing of the demands of each side while demonstrating that accepting the negotiated package will create gains for all. If the negotiation formula can introduce elements of good governance and integrity to counteract a heritage of corruption, all the better.

Negotiations are most likely to find an interested audience if the conflict has reached a ripe moment. As Zartman pointed out, there are moments in the life cycles of conflicts which, if seized, will result in successful resolution of conflicts and a return to an acceptable order.[19] What makes a conflict ripe for resolution are "mutually hurting stalemates," that is, perceptions of increasingly painful conditions that will yield only further pain and ultimately catastrophe for the conflicting parties if they are left to fester, and "mutually enticing opportunities," that is, a vision or promise of overwhelming reward or benefit. These can be incentives for decision makers to negotiate and search for mutually acceptable solutions. At the ripe moment, along with hurting stalemates or rewarding opportunities, the parties must also be able to see a way out of the conflict. They must have a vision of a feasible and peaceful outcome that can be achieved through negotiation or mediation; this vision typically is embodied as a "negotiation formula" and can include a prominent anticorruption perspective.

Corruption Risks and Statebuilding after Conflict

The weak and fragile condition of societal structures, government institutions, and economic systems after conflict, multiplied by the vulnerability of a newly established peace and the ever-present threat of renewed violence, make rebuilding countries particularly susceptible to all types of corrupt behaviors.

Corruption takes three major forms. Petty or administrative corruption is often widespread, affecting all citizens when, for example, unofficial fees are charged for public services, items are sold on the black market, and ghost workers pad government payrolls. These practices can generate public cynicism and mistrust of the authorities, as well as a culture of lawlessness that can cause a relapse to earlier violence. Grand corruption typically involves high-level officials and the exchange of large sums of money and resources or other competitive advantages. It often manifests as outright theft of public funds, steering government contracts to family or friends, and various forms of patronage—that is, cronyism, nepotism, and political favoritism. It can divert crucial funds away from rebuilding states recently ravaged by

---

19. I. William Zartman, "Ripeness: The Hurting Stalemate and Beyond," in Stern and Druckman, eds., *International Conflict Resolution after the Cold War,* 228 and 241.

war. Finally, state capture by economic interests highlights the influence of private business on state power and collusion with public officials to extract advantage. This can be the most insidious form of corruption for rebuilding states because it diverts needed assets to an elite few and limits economic growth from diversifying across many stakeholders.

Postconflict states pose a unique set of problems concerning corruption. Some even say it is unrealistic to deal with corruption issues under most postconflict conditions because these states generally lack the minimum requirements for effective remedies; often, they are plagued by weak security situations, factionalized societal relationships, a breakdown in the rule of law, minimal administrative infrastructure to deliver services, and a lack of mechanisms to generate and assert legitimate authority.[20] Corruption can be unintentionally institutionalized into peacebuilding and reconstruction initiatives. The rapid influx of large sums of relief and development funds can be difficult to monitor and control, and thus become a target for abuse.[21] As well, in the initial shift from coercive to more open political systems after a conflict, corrupt activities may be energized. Clientelism, vote buying, misappropriation of public funds, and abuse of state resources can thrive because the rules and institutions that ensure accountability and guard against impunity are too immature. Also, the transition to a liberal market economy after conflict and insufficiently regulated privatization can create new opportunities for grand corruption and the unlawful grabbing of state assets by well-placed political elites.

Some analysts even view the potential development of such a corrupt state as a welcome and temporarily stabilizing occurrence in the statebuilding process, as greasing the wheels through bribery can keep essential services flowing and help businesspeople overcome cumbersome regulations, promoting economic activity under tenuous circumstances. Corruption can improve efficiency even if social benefits are not sacrificed for the personal benefits of a few.[22] The mutual incentives of corrupt exchange can even bring together formerly opposed groups into durable multiethnic coalitions that

---

20. Soniya Carvalho, *Engaging with Fragile States: An IEG Review of World Bank Support to Low-Income Countries under Stress* (Washington, DC: World Bank, 2006).

21. See Philippe Le Billon, "Corrupting Peace? Corruption, Peacebuilding and Reconstruction," paper submitted for future special issue of *Singapore Journal of Tropical Geography,* 2007. In addition, for an analysis of controls used to ensure proper oversight of USAID programs in crisis situations where massive and rapid rollout of funds is necessary, see Jonathan Sleeper, "How USAID Safeguards against Corruption can be used by the Millennium Challenge Account," US Agency for International Development, Issue Brief no. 3 (PN-ACT-341), Washington, DC, June 2003.

22. Maxim Mironov, "Bad Corruption, Good Corruption, and Economic Growth," unpublished paper, University of Chicago, 2005, www.mironov.fm/research/corruption.pdf (accessed July 18, 2010).

reduce the possibility of violence.[23] Political and economic elites who seek to protect their kleptocracy can impose strict controls on society to support their new order, suppressing spoilers who threaten the peace. However, if this occurs, the stability and order that such a corrupt state brings can put democratic goals on the back burner.

---

23. Robert Hislope, "When Being Bad Is Good: Corrupt Exchange in Divided Societies," paper presented at conference entitled Postcommunist States and Societies, Syracuse University, Syracuse, NY, September 30–October 1, 2005.

2

Negotiation and Development Assistance in Postconflict Settings

A country's inherent instability after conflict—its inadequate governance institutions and minimal accountability and transparency—provides an ideal breeding ground for corrupt behavior. Corruption, in turn, weakens governance even further, depriving the state of needed revenues to provide adequate services and controls and scaring away investors. Ill-gotten funds in the hands of spoiler factions can be funneled to insurgents, resulting in a spiral of ever-increasing violence.

It is better to deal with the problem of possible corruption very early in the postconflict period; negotiating good governance provisions in the initiating peace accords or in early development assistance programs can control corruption before it becomes a predictable everyday transaction. In transformational countries, incentives that promote accountability and transparency need to be introduced early, as institutions and the rule of law are being strengthened or rebuilt. If action is not taken very early in reconstruction, it may become difficult, if not impossible, to turn the tide of corruptive behavior.

My principal hypothesis is that a durable peace and economic recovery in countries emerging from violent conflict are more likely to occur and be sustainable if corruption vulnerabilities are addressed effectively in the conflict-ending negotiations, or soon after by development assistance programs. Given this hypothesis, the study examines two key questions. First, how can negotiation processes that end conflict also generate fundamental provisions of anticorruption and good governance so that these emerging societies are better prepared to cope with economic recovery—and what motivates discussion of these provisions in the peace negotiation process? Second, what development assistance initiatives can governments, international donors, and NGOs take early to enhance the effects of negotiated anticorruption measures or, in their absence, to change the perverse incentive structure of corruption? Does the timing of such initiatives make a difference?

The prospects for long-term resolution of violent conflict that yields stability and growth often emerge from a complex multistage process. Peace agreements are achieved principally through negotiations, which provide the process by which conflicting parties come together to devise a joint vision of a peaceful future, resolving issues to end the violence and, perhaps, the conflict, and to arrive at formal agreements. But it takes intricate postagreement efforts to ensure that the commitments the parties made in negotiations are realized. How the agreement is implemented—with what speed, with what resources, and with what political will by all parties—will directly affect the success of conflict resolution.

Negotiation

Negotiating efforts to resolve conflicts can be deconstructed into several key building blocks that assess who participates, within what parameters, using what techniques, and with what results.[1] Peace negotiations are particularly sensitive examples of this process because of the environment of violence, long-term grievances, and stakes at risk—as shown by the peace negotiations in El Salvador, Guatemala, Sierra Leone, Burundi, Papua New Guinea, and Liberia, each of which are analyzed in detail in this volume.

Which *actors* are involved in peace negotiations often reflects directly on the eventual success of the process. Suspicions can run high if the government is represented by officials who are alleged to be corrupt. Can they be expected to be trustworthy negotiating partners? On the rebel side, it is usually the goal to include all factions, to ensure that all parties participate in the discussions and buy in to the ultimate agreement. By leading and forming coalitions within the negotiation process, local actors can focus their efforts, build and exercise power, and influence the path toward agreement. In the Papua New Guinea talks, for example, the rebel factions coalesced in the negotiation stage, speaking with a unified voice and thus maximizing their demands. In Sierra Leone, the rebels were so much better prepared for the talks than the government that their demands were quickly incorporated into the ultimate agreement. Factions that are excluded or decide on their own not to participate in negotiations can become spoilers of the eventual peace. In Burundi,

---

1. See Victor Kremenyuk, ed., *International Negotiation: Analysis, Approaches, Issues,* 2nd ed. (San Francisco, CA: Jossey Bass, 2002).

several rebel factions remained at the margins or out of the talks altogether, continuing to make demands after the peace agreement was signed.

Local factions are not the only ones that participate in peace negotiations; neighboring countries, countries with a special interest in the conflict, and regional and international organizations can also be drawn into the conflict and its resolution, either as supporters of particular factions or as mediators and donors. They can apply significant pressure or offer meaningful rewards to local actors to end the violence and resolve differences. In Sierra Leone and El Salvador, donors promised extensive development assistance if the parties made difficult concessions quickly. In Liberia, the international presence strongly influenced not only the proceedings, but the agreement's contents.

Negotiations assume particular *structures* that set physical and organizational parameters within which the process operates. For example, most peace negotiations are multiparty; often many factions and external actors want a seat at the negotiating table. The balance of power among these parties can vary widely, but when there is power symmetry across negotiating actors, that is generally found to improve the chances of finding a consensus to end conflict. In El Salvador, negotiations were entered into with an explicit parity between the rebels and the civilian government. In Guatemala's prolonged negotiations, a sense of balance and equality developed between the rebels and the military as informal talks diminished common suspicions and yielded a sense of mutual trust.

The organization of the negotiation also is important. Some negotiations are held in secret to enable parties to state their interests with greater candor and disavow potentially embarrassing concessions that might not come to fruition. On the other hand, full and open talks mitigate backroom deals among more powerful actors to the detriment of others. The strong participation of civil society in the Guatemalan negotiations made a major difference in finding an inclusive settlement. Because peace negotiations are typically so complex, involving many issues and grievances, they often are organized into several issue-specific committees or work groups, which help to divide the larger problem into more resolvable elements, as in the Burundi process.

The negotiation *process* for complex peace talks is usually multistaged, involving face-to-face talks around a negotiating table as well as off-line private talks to resolve key sticking issues. Mediation by an outside power is often a major feature, a catalyst for principal opponents to begin talks and an engine to keep the talks moving. In El Salvador, mediator-imposed deadlines sped the process toward resolution. The timing and pace of negotiations also relate to relative success in achieving agreements. A history of earlier negotiations, perhaps failed or incomplete, can help spur on the peace process, allowing it to avoid previous pitfalls and include earlier partial agreements, as in Guatemala. In Liberia, the negotiation process was spurred by imminent rebel attacks on the capital as the talks were proceeding, inducing a hurting stalemate and a process ripe for resolution.

Perhaps the most important aspect of a negotiation is the way specific *issues* are considered. Which issues are to be tackled in negotiations? Ought there be a proper balance between stopping the violence and developing the basis for a stable peace? Ending the fighting can involve not only a cease-fire and demobilization of forces, but finding a way to right past wrongs and seeking redress and accountability for grievances. Zartman and Kremenyuk call this an issues platform for seeking justice, a backward-looking outcome.[2] Alternatively, a forward-looking set of issues seeks to establish a stable situation in which the underlying causes of the conflict have been resolved. This usually involves establishing new paths for governance. Integrating both forward- and backward-looking goals is not necessarily contradictory, but requires a multi-issue formula that incorporates balance, imagination, creativity, and political will by all actors to address past, immediate, and longstanding causes of the conflict. In an inventory of peace agreements negotiated between 1980 and 2006, Vinjamuri and Boesenecker found that fifty-four out of seventy-seven accords (70 percent) included justice provisions.[3] Among these, most common were provisions dealing with general amnesty for rebels, prisoner releases, and police reform—primarily backward-looking elements—rather than more comprehensive and forward-looking governance items dealing with judicial system reform.

A forward-looking formula requires a holistic examination of the conflict and paths toward its solution. For internal conflicts, a workable formula often requires the government to accept the rebels' grievances—what they believe initiated the conflict—and to adopt some of the rebels' demands to resolve the conflict. Such negotiation formulas involve the development of a new relationship among former combatants, along with new mechanisms to deal with their problems, to achieve long-term peace with justice. In El Salvador, for instance, both sides found they had a common enemy in the armed forces, which pointed the way to an agreeable formula.

Zartman and Kremenyuk's review of twelve cases suggests that peace negotiations based on forward-looking formulas were more likely to yield

---

2. I. William Zartman and Victor Kremenyuk, eds., *Peace versus Justice.*

3. Leslie Vinjamuri and Aaron Boesenecker, *Accountability and Peace Agreements: Mapping Trends from 1980 to 2006* (Geneva: Centre for Humanitarian Dialogue, 2007).

stable conflict settlements, while those with primarily backward-looking formulas failed to produce long-term results.[4] In these latter cases, conflict tended to reemerge because the roots of the conflict remained unresolved. Analysis of the processes that resulted in forward-looking formulas suggests that all parties need to decide early to share in a new approach to the negotiation, sometimes motivated by an outside mediator. Conflict ripeness—local parties' perceptions of a mutually hurting stalemate—can produce movement toward forward-looking outcomes. In addition, a mutual recognition of former foes, an end to the fighting, a change of attitudes, and a vision of the future as a common project can orient negotiators toward dealing with the underlying conflict issues, establishing a new regime with effective governance institutions and processes and accountability for past wrongs.

Negotiation *strategies* in peace talks revolve around the actors' use of power. Are their strategies aimed at persuading others to concede (contending strategies), reducing aspirations (yielding strategies), or locating the point where all or most goals can be satisfied (problem-solving strategies)?[5] Integrative bargaining strategies, by which parties seek ways for all to believe they have satisfied their objectives, are the path toward long-lasting stability after peace agreements are negotiated.

Negotiated *outcomes* in peace talks are invariably complex, balancing multiple issues, actors, promises, and commitments within a proposed schedule of implementation. The perceived fairness of the negotiated agreement depends on how it handles past, present, and future problems and the extent to which its underlying formula, in its approach, integrates the interests of all former combatants.

Development Assistance

After the negotiated agreement is hashed out, the hard work of making it a reality must be accomplished for the benefits of peace to be realized. In most cases, the initial focus is on ensuring a cease-fire, demobilization, peacekeeping, and reconstruction. These efforts help to create an atmosphere in which real development can be initiated; broader and more comprehensive implementation assistance often is made available after security has been established. Often, though not always, implementation assistance is patterned after the provisions of the negotiated agreement.

---

4. Zartman and Kremenyuk, eds., *Peace versus Justice.*
5. Dean Pruitt, "Strategy in Negotiation," in Kremenyuk, ed., *International Negotiation.*

The major engine for implementation is international development assistance by foreign donors, some of whom may have been involved in the peace negotiations. Reintegrating former combatants, rebuilding the economic infrastructure, establishing the rule of law and political institutions, and strengthening capacity to deliver public services usually depends on donors for resources and technical assistance. Development assistance from donors is likely to be forthcoming especially if the negotiated agreement includes specific provisions related to these issues of governance and regime strengthening.In Sierra Leone, international donors took more ownership for implementing governance reforms after the peace agreement than the government, which showed a distinct lack of political will. When donors perceive minimal political will or resources, or political interference from governments, their enthusiasm for promoting reform recedes, as in Guatemala, Burundi, and Liberia. In the face of vague peace provisions, on the other hand, slow or partial donor programs can bog down the implementation process, as in El Salvador's judicial reforms.

Often, donors are involved in the negotiation process itself and may have a say in formulating these future governance provisions. Immediately after the signing of a peace agreement, pledge conferences are typically held to generate broad support for the agreement and accumulate the resources needed for implementation. If physical security can be established quickly and the political will exists to implement the agreement provisions, there can be a quick ramp-up of development assistance. This is often the case after natural disasters and emergencies, but also has been witnessed after peace agreements.[6] Massive assistance efforts are vulnerable to mishandling and corruption, but with careful control and auditing procedures, they can be implemented in a relatively efficient and effective way.

Development assistance after conflict is subject to many other operational problems, related to effective donor coordination, the speed of implementation, the full availability of resources pledged, integration with the activities of the host government, cultural compatibility, and awareness and availability of best practices. A counterpoint to these circumstances occurred in Papua New Guinea, where donor support was programmed and implemented vigorously for a ten- to fifteen-year period until the agreed-upon referendum for independence. But donors generally lack the patience to see their implementation activities through to the end. They fear being trapped in a quagmire of postconflict instability, get distracted by other issues, or lack

---

6. Sleeper, "USAID Safeguards against Corruption."

the funding to finish the job, as was the case in Burundi and Guatemala. While development assistance provided to postconflict countries is essential to implement the negotiated peace provisions, its execution is typically haphazard, uncoordinated, underfunded, and shortsighted.

Monitoring Change

There are several ways to evaluate the above hypothesis by comparing real-world cases. The dynamics and outcomes of negotiation and development assistance can be observed and assessed qualitatively, as I do in the six conflict cases below. More quantitatively, the results of negotiations and development assistance can be monitored using aggregate indicators to determine if change in the expected direction was achieved.

The World Bank's control of corruption indicator provides an annual point of reference for country corruption levels. I anticipate that countries emerging from conflict that proceed effectively through negotiation and development assistance stages with special emphasis on anticorruption and good governance improvements show a boost in their control of corruption scores—more so than a control group. The average change for 200 countries over a recent five-year period (2003–08) is very small and negative (−0.2 percent), though a very small number of countries show great improvement (up to 19 percent) and some show great declines (up to −22 percent). Given these findings, a change of even 5 percent or more over a five-year period could be seen as impressive.

Similarly, several years after a peace agreement, increases in another relevant World Bank indicator—political stability—would be evidence of sustained and controlled improvement. Between 2003 and 2008, the variance in political stability scores across all countries remained almost unchanged (average difference of −0.1 percent) with a maximum improvement of 25 percent and a maximum decline of −26 percent for a very few countries. So again, even a modest change in this indicator suggests significant improvement. I use these indicators in the cases to assess the extent of potential gains of negotiating anticorruption provisions into peace agreements.

Analytical Structure of the Book

My research is organized around several important assumptions that can shed light on both the negotiation and implementation dynamics that lead to sustainable peace treaties. First, corruption and bad governance practices can be potent grievances at the root cause of violent internal conflicts, and these grievances need to be addressed and resolved within peace agreements to attain forward-looking solutions. Including explicit anticorruption and good governance provisions in agreements can be the path to reversing the negative effects of these grievances. Accountability, transparency, and integrity standards in negotiated peace provisions that promote predictable democratic governance in accordance with the rule of law can yield long-term stability by dealing proactively with the core issues that initiated the conflict. Second, I assume that negotiation is the prominent mechanism by which the conflicting parties and interested mediating parties can promote peaceful outcomes. However, development assistance from donors is also essential to strengthen the capacity of local stakeholders to implement negotiated provisions and promote local ownership.

Another way of articulating the argument—our central proposition—revolves around the assumed beneficial effect of integrity provisions in the peace agreement. Dealing with key underlying causes of the conflict, such as corruption and governance abuses, can be vital in both resolving the conflict and sustaining the peace by providing a forward-looking outcome, in which those abuses have been eliminated and improved approaches to governance have been embedded to replace them.

To test this proposition, one needs to examine several questions. How are integrity provisions negotiated into agreements? What form do these integrity provisions take in the agreement? Are the provisions typically put into practice as anticipated during the peace implementation period? What are the means by which they are implemented? Do these provisions, if implemented adequately, reduce corruption, improve governance, and sustain the peace? Finally, what lessons have been learned from past cases that can improve the negotiation and implementation processes in future peace talks concerning internal conflicts?

I analyze examples of recent internal conflicts resolved through negotiation with the above questions in mind. My sample consists of six cases—Burundi (Arusha Agreement, August 28, 2000), El Salvador (Chapultepec Agreement, January 16, 1992), Guatemala (December 29, 1996), Liberia (Accra Agreement, August 18, 2003), Papua New Guinea (Bougainville Agreement, August 30, 2001), and Sierra Leone (Lomé Agreement, July 7, 1999)—in which peace agreements were negotiated with good governance provisions to determine how and why anticorruption issues were actively incorporated into the peace talks and what came of them. Each of the cases involves a negotiated resolution of internal conflicts where issues of corruption and integrity played a large role during the talks and in the outcome of the negotiations. The sample was drawn from the inventory of cases in the U.S. Institute of Peace (USIP) Peace Agreements Digital Collection and the International Conflict Research Institute (INCORE) list of peace agreements. Cases were selected if they satisfied several criteria: the conflicts were concluded through negotiated agreements; the resulting outcomes yielded a stable peace; governance and anticorruption provisions were explicitly included in the negotiated agreement; there was adequate and accessible information on the negotiation process, implementation, and corruption outcomes; and the cases represented geographic diversity across regions.

In addition to the analysis of the negotiated peace process, I also review and analyze the development assistance programs and postagreement negotiations conducted to implement these six peace agreements to assess the extent to which these efforts helped to establish a lasting peace. Lastly, I examine several quantitative indicators of corruption control and political and economic growth for the six cases, comparing them with the same indicators for seven cases in which peace agreements were arrived at without good governance provisions. Even though the sample is quite small, the comparison reveals a distinct and positive trend in outcomes for postconflict countries that put reestablishing integrity high on their agendas. Based on this multistaged analysis, I offer practical guidance for negotiators, diplomats, and international development professionals, including more effective ways to reduce corruption early in the postconflict period.

Part I:
Cases

Cases

Corruption can significantly damage both future political and economic development and peace prospects for countries emerging from conflict. Likewise, the fragility of the rebuilding context after conflict can seriously influence the growth of corruption, completing a vicious circle that exacerbates the vulnerabilities of the state and destabilizes the new peace. If governing structures, procedures, and the rule of law remain fragile and corruption runs rampant, development gains may be hampered, divisiveness within society may continue, spoiler factions may be emboldened, and conflict can reignite, resulting in renewed chaos and human suffering.

Finding ways to fight corruption and corruptive influences under transitional circumstances, while challenging, is not impossible. If there is recognition of the core problems and the will to deal with them, coupled with the resources and internal and external demand to tackle them forthrightly, progress can be made.

From peacebuilding to statebuilding, much happens in countries emerging from conflict that shapes their democratic, governance, and economic foundations and outlook. It begins with the negotiation process that ends the conflict and continues through the implementation of negotiated provisions. The nature of the peace agreement is crucial to the future development of integrity and stability. This depends on whether the agreement provisions address only the immediate cessation of violence or recognize the need to deal with some of the initiating, deeply rooted causes of the conflict and the inherent instability of the postconflict period.

I selected six recent cases of peace negotiations—Burundi, El Salvador, Guatemala, Liberia, Papua New Guinea, and Sierra Leone—because they incorporated good governance and anticorruption provisions explicitly into their negotiation processes. I do not completely describe the overall negotiation process; rather, I focus on those actors, strategies, processes, institutions, and dynamics that helped to produce anticorruption provisions in the negotiated agreements. The cases are presented in chronological order.

Following a brief summary of the conflict, each case is presented in a parallel fashion, dealing with the agreement's anticorruption provisions, the negotiation process that enabled the agreement, an analysis of that process, the agreement's implementation, and the midterm effects of these processes on controlling corruption after the agreement was signed. The exact language of the anticorruption and good governance provisions as they appear in the negotiated agreements are excerpted in the annex.

3

El Salvador

The civil war in El Salvador lasted eleven years, between 1981 and 1992. Insurgents from five movements under the banner of the Frente Farabundo Martí de Liberación Nacional (FMLN) waged a guerrilla struggle against military-dominated regimes in San Salvador.[1] By the end of the bloody and destructive conflict, at least 75,000 civilians had been killed, 8,000 more were missing, a million were left homeless, and another million were exiled. The government's bombing raids, atrocities, massacres, human rights abuses, and harsh repression of dissent were well publicized.

Injustices ran the gamut from land allocation inequities, election fraud, economic inequalities, suspension of constitutional rights, and an ineffective and corrupt judicial system to unaccountable police. An alliance had formed between the military and the agro-export elite, who controlled the government and needed powerful support to maintain their economic dominance. In addition to outright repression, the military exhibited aggressive rent-seeking behavior in what some label a corrupt, protection-racket state, to use Stanley's term.[2] The peasants mobilized under a banner of liberation theology, questioning the legitimacy of the state's authoritarian institutions, their corruption and lack of accountability. The government responded with more repression rather than meaningful reform.

The Christian Democrats, who dominated the government after a 1979 reformist coup, instituted some reforms, including a land reform program and nationalization of the banking, coffee, and sugar-export industries. The

---

1. Additional sources for each of the cases are listed in Annex 1.

2. William Stanley, *The Protection Racket State: Elite Politics, Military Extortion, and Civil War in El Salvador* (Philadelphia: Temple University Press, 1996).

FMLN rejected these as superficial when human rights abuses and death squads continued and it was clear that the government was still beholden to the military's influence. The right-wing parties and economic elite, championed by the Alianza Republicana Nacionalista (ARENA) party, also opposed the reform programs, as they appeared to threaten their own interests.

The Christian Democrats could not restrain the abuses of the armed forces, achieve military victory over the guerrillas, achieve peace, or improve the economy, and the war had come to a military stalemate. Moreover, widespread corruption was commonly viewed as the modus operandi of government. In the 1989 presidential election, the ARENA party candidate, Alfredo Cristiani, won office with a platform of maintaining some of the reforms previous governments had already instituted, attacking the problems of malnutrition and illiteracy, which were seen as among the root causes of the civil war, instituting free market and privatization solutions to boost the economy, and negotiating with the rebels. According to national opinion polls at the time, over 83 percent of the population favored a negotiated settlement to the war. There had been periodic attempts to negotiate earlier, but both the government and the rebel FMLN walked away from the table to continue the military conflict.

The FMLN's November 1989 military offensive and the army's murder of six Jesuit priests were critical turning points. A military stalemate was obvious and both sides preferred a political negotiated settlement to continued inconclusive fighting.

The Negotiated Agreement

The Peace Agreement between the government of El Salvador and the Frente Farabundo Martí para la Liberación Nacional (FMLN) was signed in Chapultepec on January 16, 1992, with 100 pages of detailed provisions and timelines, many dedicated to the underlying causes of the conflict, including governance and corruption abuses. In addition to implementing an immediate cease-fire, the agreement covers a range of political, economic, and social reforms that need to be made, including agrarian and land-tenure reforms. It emphasizes the transformation of the FMLN into a political party and ensures its participation in government through reintegration.

Several provisions in the agreement specifically relate to good governance and anticorruption reforms. These reforms target the armed forces, national police, and judiciary to strengthen their professionalism through improved training and oversight mechanisms. The parties affirmed that the National

Council of the Judiciary should maintain strict independence from other organs of government and from political parties so that judicial selection can be free from undue political pressure and abuse of power. The decision was made to establish a judicial training school to ensure improvements in the professional training of judges and other judicial officials. An office of the human rights ombudsman was established as an independent body, elected by the legislative assembly to defend victims of human rights abuse and corruption.

The Negotiation Process

The military-political alliance under the Christian Democrats had been the engine of war and repression. After Cristiani's election in 1989, both sides to the conflict—the ARENA-led government under President Cristiani and the FMLN—were anxious to diminish the army's political role and influence. The political leadership of government allied with the country's economic elite to force the military to back down so that the civilian economic forces could again wield power. For the FMLN, reducing army abuses and the military's unchecked political influence would resolve many of their grievances.

The confluence of interests with the change in government in 1989 generated a workable formula to resolve the conflict. By pushing for the military's reduced influence, the government successfully convinced the FMLN to join peace negotiations and initiate compromises.[3] These parties' shared interests went to the core of the conflict, and trade-offs appeared possible concerning the overhaul of civilian-military relations.

With UN mediation support, twenty-two months of negotiations began in early 1990. The negotiation goals of the FMLN included reintegrating rebel members into the political and institutional life of the country, through political activities, the national civil police, and agricultural production. The early government agenda for negotiations began with establishing a ceasefire first, then promoting constitutional and socioeconomic reforms, including the electoral system, human rights, the judicial system, and restructuring the armed forces. But the talks stalemated on the issues of purging the army and impunity for human rights abuses. Proposals were discussed to establish a civilian inspector-general for the armed forces to introduce accountability.

---

3. The FMLN had forged a close alliance with an unarmed political movement years earlier, known as the Revolutionary Democratic Front (FDR). Together, they favored democratic processes and the idea of finding a negotiated solution to the conflict. Their negotiation strategy had been developed as far back as 1982. Joaquin Villalobos, "The Salvadorean Insurgency: Why Choose Peace?" *Accord* 16 (2005).

In April and May 1990, to speed up the talks, the original plan to negotiate a cease-fire first, followed by negotiation of all other outstanding issues, was scrapped. This was an important concession from the government. Issues were subdivided and negotiated separately. But talks quickly deadlocked once again—from mid-1990 to April 1991—on the issue of reforming the armed forces. Smaller agreements on establishing a UN human rights verification mission to investigate abuses sustained the negotiations over this period and kept up a sense of momentum.

By 1991, the assembly had passed several historical reforms to the constitution, which raised expectations that a negotiated agreement was finally within reach. In addition, both sides viewed the rapidly approaching retirement in December 1991 of UN Secretary-General Javier Pérez de Cuéllar—the overseer of the negotiations—as a major deadline, stimulating rapid resolution in the talks. In April 1991, negotiations on constitutional reforms resulted in an agreement to circumscribe the army's role in politics, remove its policing functions, and establish strengthened civilian institutions to provide controls and accountability. The agreement's creation of a more accountable civilian police force, previously within the military's domain, was one attempt to institutionally limit the armed forces' autonomy and influence by constitutionally redefining them. In addition, a more autonomous judiciary, independent of executive and legislative influence, was provided with a separate budget. An interparty commission was formed to negotiate electoral and judicial reforms. These negotiations were facilitated by the UN secretary-general's representative and spurred on by pressure from the United States and the waning Soviet Union. The United States promised extensive political and financial support in the closing days of the negotiation for postwar reconstruction and the FMLN's political integration if an agreement was reached that especially reduced the political influence of the armed forces.

The negotiation process largely turned on the shared interest in minimizing the military's role. Cristiani could extract major concessions from the army and compel them to comply. If the FMLN had not appeared as interested in compromise as they did, this government position might have been a riskier foray. At the same time, the economic elite perhaps felt more threatened by the military than the rebels. By democratizing, Cristiani retained power and controlled the army. The army, for its part, accepted this condition because they trusted the president could extend extensive military aid from the United States, which was threatened by the end of Ronald Reagan's presidency.

Negotiation Analysis

One of the key drivers of the negotiated settlement was the reassertion of oligarchic authority over the armed forces. A peace agreement became possible because of the evolving relationships among the economic elite, coffee entrepreneurs, and the armed forces, which coincided with the rebel's interests in limiting the military's influence and authority. A basic negotiation formula became possible with the ascension of Cristiani to the presidency: reducing the influence and autonomy of the armed forces to accede to the interests of both the ARENA government and the FMLN rebels. This left open the door to resolve many other issues.

The negotiations were made possible because the FMLN and the government sat at the table with relative negotiating parity. Power symmetry was an essential feature, allowing both sides to make the concessions necessary to reach agreement. The structure of the negotiation process helped to define the issues and reach agreements. UN mediation was a critical agent of momentum. Finally, the practice of splitting larger issues into smaller, more manageable pieces—in essence, a divide-and-conquer strategy—worked. Issues were considered separately and solutions found within each issue domain. Setting deadlines in the negotiations also spurred progress and results. In the end, both sides believed that they had won, and reforms that produced full-fledged democracy were negotiated, while limiting the exercise of executive power.

Implementation

At the time the accords were signed in 1992, UN Secretary-General Boutros Boutros-Ghali said that "the agreement constitutes a prescription for a revolution by negotiation." Not only was the military subordinated to civilian authority, but the independence of the judiciary was asserted, economic and social questions addressed, a commission on truth established, and the Office of the Human Rights Ombudsman created. Within two years of signing the accord, the guerrilla forces were demobilized and transformed into a political party and initial elections were conducted. Since then, the cease-fire between the government and rebels has not been broken. Five years after the peace accords, an end to violent conflict and demilitarization had largely been accomplished and a wide opening to democratic participation had taken place. But detailed compliance with the accords has been mixed.

Several major elections have occurred after the accords, but voter turn-out has declined over time. Structural reforms in the electoral system were not implemented. The ARENA party lost in the municipal and legislative elections in 1997, many say, because of internal infighting and corruption scandals. Moreover, the national economy deteriorated between 1992 and 1997. Implementation of judicial reforms and the ombudsman office was hampered by lack of trust, skepticism, and lack of political will by top-ranking authorities, including the minister of public security and the head of the National Civilian Police (PNC). They sabotaged reform efforts by seeding public doubt, accusing the judges and ombudsman themselves of fostering crime and corruption. By promoting this suspicion, they poisoned the environment that was supposed to strengthen these institutions and instill respect for the rule of law. In addition, budgetary increases meant to strengthen the institutions were reduced by the government instead.

The new PNC suffered from deficiencies in its internal control mechanisms and inspector-general oversight functions, leading to mixed results:

> Nine years after the accords were signed, the PNC was more humane and account-able than the old security forces. In contrast to the past, PNC officers accused of torture, killings, vigilante activities, and excessive use of force were subject to internal sanctions and to judicial prosecution. The PNC was a more transparent and civilian-controlled institution than any of its predecessors, though it was rife with many of the same faults. Corruption was widespread, fueled by inconsistent and weak internal disciplinary procedures and by a government decision to sacrifice selection standards in order to attract and deploy more police agents in 1996 and 1997.[4]

As mentioned above, the accords had included the establishment of the National Human Rights Ombudsman Office independent of the executive branch, to investigate complaints and recommend sanctions against abusive public servants. The office was created by law in 1991 but positions were not filled until after the accord was signed. The Dutch, Swedish, Norwegian, and Finnish governments provided financial support through UNDP. The United Nations also provided technical assistance for institution building. In 1995, with the selection of a new human rights advocate and support from the UN Observer Mission in El Salvador (ONUSAL), the office actively issued reports on violations and investigated complaints against the police, judiciary, and military.

Judicial reforms in the accords were agreed upon quickly at the end of the negotiations, but were not very specific. After the new government and

---

4. Charles T. Call, "Assessing El Salvador's Transition from Civil War to Peace," in Stephen Stedman, Donald Rothchild, and Elizabeth Cousens, eds., *Ending Civil Wars: The Implementation of Peace Agreements* (Boulder, CO: Lynne Rienner Publishers, 2002), 402.

legislature took office in mid-1994, some of the accord's provisions began to be implemented. A new supreme court was elected according to new and more transparent and inclusive constitutional provisions that were passed as part of the peace process. A review of judges began in 1994 that resulted in investigations, suspensions, and sanctions of lower-court judges. However, public opinion polls taken in 1997 revealed that the public still had little trust in the judiciary. The judicial system remains weak, partisan, and subject to corruption. The vague provisions for judicial reform in the peace accords and political infighting resulted in a stalemate of legal reforms.

Postagreement donor assistance programs focused on supporting implementation of the negotiated governance and anticorruption provisions. Highlights of some of these programs include the following:[5]

- **Private sector reforms.** Programs supported constructive discussions about corruption in the private sector and produced recommendations for future anticorruption measures and action plans to generate regional networking and institutionalized anticorruption efforts, especially aimed to benefit small- and medium-sized enterprises; sponsored by Deutsche Gesellschaft für Technische Zusammenarbeit (GTZ, Germany) with Transparency International from 2002–05.
- **Local governance support.** The Municipal Development and Citizen Participation Project (1993–99) supported municipal finance and management, citizen participation in local governance, and policy dialogue and reform; sponsored by USAID.
- **Parliamentary support.** Programs provided legislators with professional advisory and training services so they could perform their tasks more effectively. They also supported local political leaders and improved relations between politicians and the electorate. Training and workshops were conducted, radio programs were produced, and advice provided at the local and national level; sponsored by the Norwegian Agency for Development Cooperation (NORAD) between 2002 and 2006.

---

5. World Bank, "Status of Projects in Execution," http://www.worldbank.org/operations/disclosure/sope.html (accessed December 7, 2010); Stephen Pereira, "Case Study: El Salvador Post Conflict Program in Democracy and Governance," Research Triangle Institute for USAID, July 2003, http://www.rti.org/pubs/El_Salvador_Case_Study.pdf (accessed December 7, 2010); USAID El Salvador, "Development Assistance Program Overview," http://www.usaid.gov/sv/development.html (accessed December 7, 2010); Call, "Assessing El Salvador's Transition;" Transparency International, "Perfil del sistema nacional de integridad de El Salvador," Costa Rica, June 2003; USAID, *Anticorruption and Transparency Coalitions: Lessons from Peru, Paraguay, El Salvador and Bolivia* (Washington, DC: USAID, 2005), http://info.worldbank.org/etools/ANTIC/docs/Resources/Country%20Profiles/Paraguay/USAID_ACTransparencyCoalitons.pdf (accessed December 7, 2010).

- **Law enforcement.** Institutional and logistic support was provided to the National Civilian Police (PNC) at police stations to enhance their capabilities and communication resources. Programs provided computer equipment and digital console tables for 911 emergency systems to strengthen case preparation and management; sponsored by USAID.
- **Civil service reform.** The public sector modernization program (1996–99) supported administrative and civil service reform, as well as tax policy and administrative improvements. E-government, consumer protection, and decentralization efforts were supported; sponsored by the World Bank.

By 2002, ten years after the accords were signed, reform of key state institutions was still far from complete. Economic growth, however, had been dramatic. After the accords, the Salvadorian economy grew at a faster rate than the average for the rest of Latin America, inflation and poverty levels fell, and literacy and infant mortality rates improved. At the same time, economic problems—many of which were at the root of the civil war—persisted, including income distribution inequalities.

Overall, there is a general perception that corruption levels in El Salvador are relatively low compared with the rest of Central America. However, clientelism and patrimonialism are still dominant in politics. There is no clear distinction between what is public or private, resulting in a government that is dominated and captured by the economic elites. Some reforms to judicial and electoral institutions were accomplished, although not completely, as planned by the accords.

Conclusions

The government of El Salvador has made some important strides in the past few years in the fight against corruption. Although prosecutions of government officials for corruption are not commonplace, some noteworthy actions to penalize public sector corruption have helped to increase public confidence in government. Recently, a former high-level official was sentenced to fifteen years in prison for fraud in awarding public services contracts and a former assembly member was stripped of immunity for allegations of bribery of local officials and money laundering.

El Salvador's peace agreement primarily focused on restoring justice and rule of law to lead the country back to democratic and peaceful development.

However, implementation of judicial reforms and the creation of the ombuds-man office were hindered by the absence of political will and popular support. Civil society in El Salvador continues to lack trust in enforcement mecha-nisms. International aid has contributed to an increase in the institutional ca-pacity of relevant agencies, but clear effects are still hard to see.

On the other hand, the World Bank control of corruption index suggests a reduction in corrupt behaviors. Between 1996 and 2000, the index shows an 8.2 percent improvement. While corruption in El Salvador is believed to be less endemic and systemic than in other Central American countries, it is still perceived as high by citizens who question the efficacy of the state's use of tax and other revenues.

One of the greatest improvements in El Salvador's anticorruption and good governance efforts can be found in the international donor support of the decentralization process that targeted transparent and accountable service delivery. The USAID Municipal Development and Citizen Participation Project generated increased involvement and mobilization of community members at a local level that promoted greater demand and distribution of resources for urban services. This assistance stimulated increased involvement of urban communities in local governance processes. The legislative develop-ment process has also progressed. El Salvador has joined the Central Ameri-can Agreement for the Prevention and Repression of Money-Laundering Crimes and implemented the relevant money-laundering and anticorruption laws through the technical and material support of USAID programs.

Since 2004, USAID, through its Transparency and Governance Program (TAG), has also supported national- and local-level anticorruption reforms and built an advocacy partnership with civil society organizations. A gov-ernment ethics tribunal has been established to lay the foundations for a heightened culture of ethical conduct and combat corruption in the public sector. In the justice sector, the attorney general's office has strengthened its anticorruption unit, the public defender's office has reassessed and enhanced its own internal procedures, the national council for the judiciary has ex-panded ethics training, and the supreme court has developed a code of ethics for judges. At the local level, international donors have promoted support for the National Commission for Local Development and the Corporation of Salvadoran Municipalities to enhance decentralization initiatives and mu-nicipal transparency.

The government has taken some steps toward strengthening the om-budsman office and restoring civilian police forces according to the peace agreement's provisions. However, to demonstrate an actual effect on corrupt behavior, more political will and pressure from civil society is still needed to institute stronger external monitoring and evaluation mechanisms. The absence of significant local participation in programs that support democratic awareness-raising and further demand for practical changes hampers progress. Donors have supported civil society organizations to build coalitions across the public and private sectors to promote transparency and accountability, but there has been limited support for the media and investigative journalism. Overall, the anticorruption and good governance provisions of the peace agreement can be said to have yielded moderately successful results.

4

Guatemala

The thirty-six-year internal war in Guatemala pitted an armed leftist insurgency against a right-wing counterinsurgent army that had coalesced with the country's economic elite. The civil war began after a failed nationalist uprising of military officers in 1960.

The rebels' grievances were many. They were mobilized against extreme socioeconomic disparities, poverty, discrimination against the indigenous population, and the impunity of the army and other government officials. Inequalities in land tenure and labor markets for Guatemala's indigenous Mayans were reflected in denials of rights to the land, political participation, and due process. Ethnic discrimination led to vast social asymmetries in the provision of health, education, and other public services. This repression of the rights of indigenous peoples, with no apparent punishment of public or military officials, was viewed as corrupt—that the leaders had abused the public trust for their own benefit. The rebels thus sought major change: land reform, tax reform, greater equity, respect for the cultural identity of the indigenous population, improved governance and public services, protection of human rights, and an end to corrupt rule and unaccountable leadership.

The war was brutal, involving massacres, assassinations, disappearances, and internal displacements. As the conflict persisted, its original causes were exacerbated. The rule of law was undermined and there was a total absence of accountability. A major offensive by the army in the late 1980s to stop the insurgents had failed and by 1990, it was obvious to all parties that the war had come to an impasse. Informal talks had begun in late 1989 with agreement to start formal negotiations in April 1991. Talks began and stalled several times over the next few years, until the United Nations was called in to officially mediate in 1994. The final agreement was signed on December

29, 1996. By the end of the conflict, approximately 200,000 civilians were dead or had disappeared.

The Negotiated Agreement

The range of long-standing grievances that initiated the conflict was ultimately addressed in the negotiated agreement, which included provisions for the observance of human rights; reconciliation with the rebels and developing a culture of peace; establishment of effective governance and participative democracy; judicial reform and respect for the rule of law; subordination of the army to civilian control; reform of public finance management; and improvement and equity in the delivery of health and education, access to land, and decentralization.

The 1996 agreement was crafted incrementally over two years, with each new agreement focused on resolving differences on a particular issue. The elements particularly related to governance and anticorruption provisions are discussed here. Starting with the Framework Agreement for the Resumption of the Negotiating Process between the Government of Guatemala and the Unidad Revolucionaria Nacional Guatemalteca (URNG) (January 10, 1994), the government and URNG, with the assistance of the UN secretary-general, agreed to resume negotiations with a UN facilitator. The framework established a general agenda and incorporated an agreement that civil society was to be central to fostering agreement and reconciliation in future negotiations. In line with this, the agreement called for a civil society assembly to discuss substantive issues in the formal negotiations, transmit their findings to the negotiators, and consider agreements reached in the formal negotiations to promote their acceptance by the wider public. The Comprehensive Agreement on Human Rights (March 29, 1994) soon followed, stating the parties' intentions to strengthen the judiciary, the Counsel for Human Rights, and the public prosecutor's office, especially to ensure their independence and strengthen the rule of law and protection of human rights. This agreement states the parties' commitment against impunity, that all who violate human rights face prosecution and punishment.

The Agreement on Social and Economic Aspects and Agrarian Situation was concluded on May 6, 1996. Here, with the most explicit reference to addressing issues of corruption, the parties agreed to promote citizen participation on social and policy issues because

> ... expanded social participation is a bulwark against corruption, privilege, distortions of development and the abuse of economic and political power to the detriment of

society.... It ensures transparency in public policies and their orientation towards the common good rather than special interests, the effective protection of the interests of the most vulnerable groups, efficiency in providing services and, consequently, the integral development of the individual.[1]

As a mechanism for greater citizen participation, the May 6 agreement resolved to reform municipal codes to establish open town council meetings and training of municipal staff in improved governance practices, as well as reestablishing local development councils that ensured citizen participation to identify local priorities. Commitments were also made to implement specific reforms in the governance of the education, health, social security, housing, labor, and agriculture sectors, as well as modernization of government services and fiscal policy—in particular, budget planning and tax administration. Also included were reforms in the auditing of public programs, the professionalization of the civil service, adoption of an Integrity and Accountability Act, and the promotion of criminal sanctions for corruption and misappropriation of public funds.

The Agreement on the Strengthening of Civilian Power and on the Role of the Armed Forces in a Democratic Society was signed on September 19, 1996. This document recognized the need to rebuild public institutions and ensure citizen participation to have true reconciliation after years of conflict. A special section of this agreement was devoted to strengthening the judicial sector: "The antiquated legal practices, slow proceedings, absence of modern office management systems and lack of supervision of officials and employees of the judicial branch breed corruption and inefficiency."[2] The need to ensure access to the justice system and reform the administration of justice to prevent the judicial branch from covering up a system of impunity and corruption was also reinforced. The agreement promoted competitive recruitment for judges, judicial discipline procedures, and reform of the penal code to recognize the serious offenses of bribery, graft, and corruption in particular. It also defined specific punishments for these acts of corruption. Modernization of the state was to be promoted through decentralizing the executive branch, attacking corruption, and strengthening the attorney general's office. Establishing a commission was recommended to ensure that these reforms of the justice system were carried forth.

---

1. From "Agreement on Social and Economic Aspects and Agrarian Situation," 1996, http://www.usip.org/files/file/resources/collections/peace_agreements/guat_960506.pdf (accessed October 19, 2010).

2. From "Agreement on the Strengthening of Civilian Power and on the Role of the Armed Forces in a Democratic Society," 1996, http://www.usip.org/files/file/resources/collections/peace_agreements/guat_960919.pdf (accessed October 19, 2010).

The agreement also recognized the need to professionalize the civil service. As part of that, it established a code of conduct, promoted legislation on integrity and accountability, ensured that the comptroller's office was strong and modern and had the necessary resources, and promoted criminal sanctions for corruption and embezzlement of public funds. Finally, the agreement clearly asserted the basic principle that the three branches of government should operate independently.

The Agreement on the Definitive Ceasefire, signed on December 4, 1996, ended the hostilities and ushered in a period of demobilization with verification. On December 7, 1996, the Agreement on Constitutional Reforms and the Electoral Regime was concluded, establishing the "fundamental basis for the reconciliation of Guatemalan society within the framework of the rule of law, democratic coexistence, full observance of and strict respect for human rights, [and] an end to impunity."[3] It included provisions for constitutional amendments to strengthen the administration of justice and careers in the judicial service. It also provided for the development of a new electoral reform commission to strengthen procedures for transparency and access to voting.

The Agreement on the Implementation, Compliance and Verification Timetable for the Peace Agreements (December 29, 1996) confirmed that the peace negotiating process had resulted in a new national agenda for overcoming the root causes of social, political, economic, ethnic, and cultural conflict and also the consequences of the armed conflict. It provided a timetable to implement most agreement activities, including governance and anticorruption initiatives, such as the modernization and decentralization of the state, public administration reform, a comprehensive strategy for rural development, and fiscal policy reforms.

The final document emerging from the peace negotiations was the Agreement on a Firm and Lasting Peace (December 29, 1996), which referenced all previous agreements and formally ended more than three decades of armed conflict in Guatemala. It emphasized the major themes of the incremental negotiation process: that a comprehensive agenda had been established to overcome the root causes of the conflict and lay the foundations for a transformed society through strengthened and just governance under the rule of law.

---

3. From "Agreement on Constitutional Reforms and the Electoral Regime," 1996, http://www.usip.org/files/file/resources/collections/peace_agreements/guat_961207.pdf (accessed October 19, 2010).

The Negotiation Process

The route of the Guatemalan negotiation process was strongly influenced by three earlier agreements; the principles embodied in them ensured that the negotiations and the ultimate agreements would deal with the underlying causes of the conflict, including governance and corruption issues. First, the Esquipulas II Central America Peace Accords of 1987 ended the Contra War in Nicaragua and created the framework for negotiations in El Salvador and Guatemala. It also established a Guatemalan national reconciliation commission and national dialogues focused on generating consensus for a negotiated settlement with social justice.

Second, talks in Oslo resulted in an accord on March 30, 1990, achieved under the auspices of the Lutheran World Federation. It brought together the URNG with the National Reconciliation Commission to come to the Basic Agreement on the Search for Peace by Political Means, which laid out future negotiation arrangements: UN monitoring, use of the commission as a conciliator, and other governance agenda items. The Oslo Accord also laid out a path for initial consultations among key stakeholders in society.

Third, when formal talks began in 1991 between the URNG and the government, preliminary agreement was reached in principle on democratization and human rights. The core negotiation formula that set forth the major principles upon which the final accord would be based was developed at talks in Mexico from April 24–26, 1991. This initial framework of the agreement set out an agenda of eleven issues to be negotiated. Most important, it established that substantive issues would be resolved before operational issues. This was a major URNG interest and demand. The government had wanted just the opposite—a cease-fire and disarmament concluded before other issues were discussed.

The civilian governments that participated in the negotiations did so seeking to build a base of power beyond the military. In doing so, they brought international attention to the negotiation process that made international norms of good governance more salient. However, the armed forces were an important stakeholder and potential spoiler. When formal talks began in 1991, the military was deeply distrustful that negotiations would resolve the conflict. However, by the final three years of talks, the army was behind the process. Some of this change in perspective was brought about by informal contacts, away from the negotiating table, between members of the military and representatives of the URNG.

Between 1991 and 1993, the government and URNG conducted negotiations under the National Reconciliation Commission's aegis, with the United Nations participating as an observer. There were few advances as both sides took very hard-line positions, and distrust was high. However, by the end of this phase, it was clear to both sides that their conflict could and would be resolved only through negotiation. Because the government refused to deal with the human rights demands of the rebels and because the president's term was ending, the negotiations ended abruptly.

However, once the negotiations got back on track in 1994, they proceeded as intended by the Mexico framework. The effects of war were discussed, human rights and resettlement issues were tackled, and a truth commission agreed upon. Between 1995 and 1996, the causes of war were discussed and formulated into substantial accords, dealing with indigenous rights, socio-economic issues, and demilitarization. Lastly, in 1996, operational accords, dealing with a cease-fire, constitutional reforms, electoral reforms, the legal and political integration of the URNG, and a timetable for the implementation of the agreements were discussed and agreed upon.

From January 1994, peace negotiations were resumed with the mediation of the United Nations, whose representative, Jean Arnault, introduced timetables and deadlines into the negotiation process. Perhaps most influential was the formation of the Mission of the United Nations in Guatemala (MINUGUA) in November 1994—it began active operations in 1995–96—as a confidence-building institution before the final accords and at a critical time in the negotiations. MINUGUA was organized to verify compliance with the peace accords through human rights and demobilization monitoring and strengthening national institutions charged with human rights protection. In addition to the United Nations, other important stakeholders were present at the negotiating table, all seeking to catalyze the talks to final resolution of the conflict. The Group of Friends—governments that wanted to see a quick resolution to the conflict[4]—formalized their role in the negotiations and represented external international pressure on the conflicting parties. A civil society assembly, not at the table, formulated proposals on contentious issues and hammered out consensus on the wide range of issues under consideration in the talks. Even though these civil society organizations did not participate formally, they were taken very seriously in the overall process of the formal negotiations. These external stakeholders to the negotiations represented the promise of the international and domestic

---

4. This group included Colombia, Norway, Mexico, Spain, the United States, and Venezuela.

community to support an ultimate accord and were a constant reminder that the world was watching.

Some initial agreements were signed in 1994, but talks slowed down the following year due to national presidential elections. By mid-1995, seeking to restart the momentum behind the talks, the consultative group of donor countries promised that major funding plans would be withheld until a final peace accord was signed and the reforms enacted.

In January 1996, a new president was elected, Alvaro Arzú, who was committed to concluding the negotiations quickly. Even before taking office, he began secret talks with the URNG and pledged to sign a final peace accord within the year, creating a climate of greater trust between the parties. He strongly recommended that the negotiating parties on both sides be reduced in size from ten persons each to four, making discussions more fluid. He was influenced by the significant international pressure, especially the threatened withholding of financial assistance. In March 1996, Arzú responded to the URNG halt of armed action with an army cease-fire. In May 1996, the Accord on Social and Economic Issues and Agrarian Situation was signed, heavily influenced by the 1992 Salvadorian peace agreement. The negotiations leading to this accord and those that followed had much to do with a change in participation at the table: the army's involvement was greatly reduced and participation by the Coordinating Committee of Agricultural, Commercial, Industrial, and Financial Associations (CACIF) was increased.

Observers could see a real transition in Guatemala from a counterinsurgency state to a participative democracy, even in the way the negotiations were conducted. There were serious consultations between civil society groups and the government, which institutionalized sincere participative approaches to decision making. The ultimate peace accord of 1996 involved major concessions from both sides, not an imposed agreement on either. The last two years of negotiations occurred in a culture of compromise, a good part of it because of the perceived power balance among the disputants, the mediating influence of the UN representative, and a sense that both sides were dealing seriously with the issues that mattered—ending not only the violence, but the initiating causes of the conflict.

Using the principles established in earlier forums, the two major stakeholders generated a political pact that outlined serious commitments to improve governance. The final accords developed a framework to transform government institutions so that they could mediate effectively the interests of previously disempowered social groups. Principles of democratic participation, consultation, and accountability were embedded and promoted in the accords, and watchdog bodies in which civilian groups had an important say were mandated to monitor the implementation of the agreement's provisions.

Negotiation Analysis

The negotiated agreement sought to end the armed conflict and dismantle the repressive governmental structure by replacing it with more open, participative, accountable, and responsive governmental structures. Amid post-conflict reconstruction, fragile rule of law, corruption, organized crime, weak political parties, deep poverty, and income inequality, the agreement also sought to provide a blueprint for good public administration and an environment for sustainable peace and democracy. Both sides saw that resolving the conflict was in their best interest and made concessions at the negotiating table. President Arzú viewed the URNG as an equal player, not as a defeated force; it was not a process of victors imposing a process or its demands on the vanquished. However, both his government and the rebels were significantly weakened players by this stage in the conflict, which would have serious implications for seeing through the implementation of many negotiated provisions as intended. The armed forces, a significant and potential spoiler in negotiations, evolved from an opponent to a proponent of negotiations, even as an agreement would drastically change their role and function. Fears and suspicions were adjusted as informal, back-channel meetings produced greater familiarity and trust. The 1994 framework agreement established basic principles, served as a negotiation formula, and subsequently guided the negotiation process. It led the parties to discuss and agree on a wide range of issues that were of concern to all and which dealt with both the causes and effects of the conflict.

Existing models of negotiation frameworks and peace agreements in neighboring countries—namely, Nicaragua and El Salvador—motivated and inspired the Guatemalan talks. Negotiations clearly sought not only to end the violence, but to look forward to alleviate the issues that were at the root of the thirty-six-year conflict: discrimination against the indigenous population, poverty, inequities, and impunity of political and military leaders. While the government insisted that a cease-fire agreement come before negotiations, the rebels demanded and succeeded in having the substantive issues dealt with before laying down arms, thus salvaging an extra degree of influence and power for them.

Formal UN mediation of the negotiations raised the stakes and made the talks irreversible. During the negotiation process, the UN mediator, Jean Arnault, gained the trust of the government and guerrillas and transformed the government proposals into language that the URNG could accept. Direct contact between the parties, especially military officers and rebel leaders, reduced mistrust about the intentions of the other side and facilitated more rapid demobilization. Promises of external assistance, pressure from neighboring and donor countries, such as the withholding of postconflict reconstruction funding, and the early establishment of international support units (MINUGUA) immediately supported and verified compliance. Civil society organizations' important role in developing detailed proposals and arriving at consensus on contentious issues fed the formal negotiations, even though they were not included at the table in a formal sense.

Implementation

The original accords included a timetable to implement all provisions within four years, but this was revised after three years to extend it for an additional four years through 2004. There were 119 commitments in the negotiated agreement. The operational provisions dealing with the cease-fire, demobilization, reintegration of combatants, and return of refugees were accomplished rather quickly. Ending combat and demobilizing the guerrillas was quick and effective, and was completed ahead of the negotiated timetable. The guerrilla movement transformed itself into a political party and competed in the 1999 elections as planned. Refugees were also repatriated. However, these were not the difficult provisions. By the time the negotiations were completed, the URNG was so weak that it did not pose a major threat. Fighting had also stopped before the final agreement was signed. To date, the violence has ended and the peace has held.

The other provisions, mostly dealing with the underlying causes of the conflict, have been only partially implemented or not implemented at all. These issues were related to making Guatemala a more democratic, equitable, and integrated society, and more contentious than the cessation of violence.

A major setback was the rejection of a package of constitutional reforms in the May 1999 referendum. The government was too weak to generate enough enthusiasm from its backers. The package would have implemented into law many significant governance elements of the peace accords dealing with indigenous rights, the role of the military, democratization, and independence of the judiciary. The timetable in the accords indicated that this reform package was to be presented to Congress within ninety days and then passed onto the voters immediately upon approval. Fifty reforms were packaged together in the referendum, but it attracted a small turnout of only 18 percent of eligible voters two-and-a-half years after the accords were signed. International donors funded extensive publicity for the referendum as well as voter education drives, but to no avail. Many stakeholders who had not been at the negotiation table—within business, political parties, civil society, and the armed forces—objected and wanted to revisit these reforms. The details of the process by which the reforms would be approved and implemented were obviously lacking. Subsequent governments could not resurrect the reform package, nor did they have the political will or demand from their constituencies; the military and business elite appear to have continued wielding sufficient power after the peace accords to quash implementation of these anticipated reforms. The democratic concept of promoting consensus-building in the implementation phase—through the referendum—turned out to yield stalemate instead of affirmation of the negotiated agreement.

Despite the agreement's provisions, the military is still heavily involved in internal security. Modernization and greater independence for the judiciary is only partly implemented. Reform plans were developed and a judicial ethics code drafted, but the system of impunity and corruption in the courts still exists.

Democratization and the participation goals of the accords have been partly achieved. Many civil society organizations now participate in special commissions outlined in the accords to discuss socioeconomic, governance, judicial, and anticorruption reform issues, but there is limited consultation when it comes to real decision making. These commissions help to mobilize extensive participation of civil society in discussing and debating these issues, but the concrete results of most of these commissions in achieving change remain questionable. Donor coordination was facilitated by the United Nations and worked well. But MINUGUA was never given a Security Council mandate, weakening the diplomatic pressures it could bring to bear on the government to implement specific peace provisions.

The implementation of the critical socioeconomic and political provisions lagged in large part because the two major parties that negotiated the peace agreement—the URNG and the National Advancement Party (PAN)—had weakened with limited popular constituencies. By 2000, the conservative Guatemalan Republican Front (FRG) opposition party won the presidential and legislative elections; it had not signed the negotiated agreement and had limited commitment to implementing its remaining provisions.

The government that formulated the agreement anticipated major opportunities of international support and financial assistance after the peace accord was signed. As a result, the agreement was developed with broad and sweeping provisions, but with few specifics to guide practical implementation and few particulars about which actors were to be held accountable for implementing provisions. Responsibilities for the accords were distributed so broadly that it slowed and blocked progress.

The efforts of major international actors providing institutional strengthening assistance after the accords—including USAID, the World Bank, and the Inter-American Development Bank—were more well-funded that those of MINUGUA. But while their assistance relates to major governance and anticorruption provisions, the Guatemalan courts, public ministry, and police have shown little willingness to strengthen judicial institutions, update criminal codes, or establish an effective office of the human rights ombudsman. Institutional vulnerabilities in these areas were major contributing factors at the start of the civil war, as those in the military and police suspected of corruption were seldom prosecuted or punished. The judiciary was also perceived to be highly corrupt, easily influenced by bribes, and poorly trained.

The peace agreement had envisioned establishing a national civilian police that would take domestic security functions from the military and make it more accountable and transparent by putting it administratively under the direction of civil authorities. The agreement also called for reforms in the administration of justice to reduce corruption, strengthen judicial ethics and independence, improve efficiency and professionalism. While the civilian police force was established by mid-2000, many of the accord's provisions concerning its structure, standards, and procedures were entirely ignored by the Guatemalan government as well as international donors, including the Spanish Civil Guard and the U.S. International Criminal Investigations Training Assistance Program (ICITAP) of the U.S. Department of Justice. Most of the justice administration provisions have never been implemented, despite many international donor programs, because the constitutional reforms were never adopted via referendum, as the Guatemalan constitution requires.

In general, the negotiated agreements provided basic principles, but were short on details for implementation. Moreover, the agreements were not backed by a broad consensus of civil society or political elites. None of the signing parties were strong enough, in the aftermath of the agreement, to deliver the political support needed to follow though on implementation, especially in the face of a new government that had not signed the agreement. While the agreements laid out an implementation procedure that promoted wide public participation and consultation, this led to a lot of discussion but no broad consensus, as had been anticipated. Where the agreements specified an implementation approach—namely, using a constitutional referendum procedure—it was difficult and unrealistic to put it into effect.

After the agreement was signed, international donors immediately provided development assistance to the Guatemalan government, hoping for rapid implementation of the accords, and their support did not flag even with the failure of the constitutional referendum. Much of the postagreement donor assistance focused on strengthening governance and anticorruption provisions of the peace treaty. Highlights of their support include the following:[5]

- **Anticorruption institutions.** Technical support was provided to rebuild national government systems for public resource management, increase devolution of authority and responsibilities to the local level, and strengthen citizen oversight of national government decision-making; sponsored by USAID between 2005 and 2009.
- **Local governance support.** The Decentralization and Local Governance Program strengthened the capacity of local governments to manage public resources, deliver basic services, and promote private-sector investment. These efforts advocated for increased resources at the local level and promoted citizen participation; sponsored by USAID between 2005 and 2009.
- **Public financial management.** These programs strengthened fiscal, financial, and fiduciary management, and improved the coverage and efficiency of social safety nets. They developed institutional capacity to manage, monitor, evaluate, and improve poverty reduction strategy

5. "USAID Guatemala Programs," http://www.usaid.gov/gt/docs/web_page_version_programs_chart.pdf (accessed December 7, 2010); "Democracy and Governance," http://www.usaid.gov/gt/democracy_governance.htm (accessed December 7, 2010); "Anticorruption, Transparency, and Accountability," http://www.usaid.gov/gt/cross_cutting.htm#anti_corruption (accessed December 7, 2010); "USAID Guatemala Programs," http://www.usaid.gov/gt/docs/usaid_gt_programs.pdf (accessed December 7, 2010). See also World Bank, "Guatemala: Projects and Programs," http://web.worldbank.org/external/default/main?menuPK=328149&pagePK=141155&piPK=141124&theSitePK=328117 (accessed December 7, 2010); Transparency International, *National Integrity Systems: Transparency International Country Report on Guatemala, 2007* (Berlin: Transparency International, 2007); Global Integrity, "Guatemala," http://www.globalintegrity.org/reports/2006/guatemala/index.cfm (accessed December 7, 2010); William David Holiday, "Broad Participation, Diffuse Responsibility: Peace Implementation in Guatemala," in *Ending Civil Wars*.

implementation. These efforts increased the effectiveness, efficiency, and transparency of the public sector financial planning, management, and control. They also supported the development and introduction of an efficient and transparent system for municipal finance management and strengthened civil participation in controlling finance management; sponsored by GTZ (Germany) from 2002 to 2005.

- **Judicial reform.** These programs supported improvements in the transparency and efficiency of criminal judicial processes through expansion of oral procedures. They supported justice centers, strengthened prosecution in corruption cases, and supported crime prevention activities. They also helped to redesign the criminal justice system and modernize and improve the functioning of the juvenile courts; sponsored by USAID and NORAD (Norway) between 2000 and 2009.

- **Electoral support.** Programs provided technical assistance and analysis, information, and international expertise necessary to effectively carry out the 2007 general elections; sponsored by NORAD (Norway) between 2006 and 2008.

- **Media and public awareness programs.** These programs supported the mass media's coverage of the peace accords and election procedures, and enhanced the functioning of independent and objective media groups; sponsored by NORAD (Norway) between 2003 and 2007.

Over time, the donors began to refocus their aid on achieving fiscal reforms, especially targeting an increase in tax revenues, rather than broader rule of law and governance reforms. Although tax collections increased, government was viewed as failing to implement these reforms effectively, and international assistance slowed.

Some lessons can be learned from the implementation process in Guatemala. First, if one or both sides to the agreement are very weak, endorsing a multidimensional peace accord may not make sense. The best situation is to maintain a strong opposition that can continue to demand implementation of the agreement after negotiations. Without this, achieving effective implementation is likely to slow down.

Second, attempts to incorporate major public participation and consultation schemes to build support for the agreement after the negotiation can yield unintended results; they can slow down or worse, deadlock implementation. In such circumstances, it is difficult for international parties to apply enough pressure to get the process moving again.

Third, peace agreements can lay the foundation for new governance procedures, but it is important for their implementation to happen quickly and reestablish competent political institutions, because international actors and donors, as well as domestic factions, have limited attention spans. The momentum of the negotiation that arrived at agreement must be sustained through implementation. The peace agreement implementation process in Guatemala sought to use traditional democratic approaches of inclusion and discussion, which turned out to be ineffective in a context that required quick and dramatic, not evolutionary, change.

Conclusions

Democratization was an essential feature of the Guatemalan agreement. Strengthening of civil society began in 1984 before peace negotiations, paving the way for the talks. In other conflicts, peace facilitates democratization reforms; Guatemala shows the opposite can also be true. Transparent elections were held, some degree of press and association freedoms were available, and civilian governments were elected years before peace negotiations began. These were necessary conditions in Guatemala to initiate peace talks.

As a result of democratic and inclusive initiatives, national debates were conducted involving many stakeholders during the implementation period on key issues of governance, indigenous questions, human rights, and the role of the military. But the ultimate decisions in the negotiations were made by a few elites and many of their agreements were not affirmed by the electorate years later.

Many actors were involved in the implementation process and there was extensive dialogue on how the implementation was to be undertaken, to the point that it slowed down the process and perhaps sabotaged it in the failed referendum. Trying to achieve consensus through give-and-take post-agreement negotiation across a wide range of stakeholders resulted in useful democratization changes, but also generated stalemate on many provisions that had been negotiated in the accords. Compliance with the accords was clearly very positive during the first few months after signing; after that, implementation clearly lagged behind the timetable or worse, stopped.

The peace agreement itemized a long list of governance and anticorruption reforms that voters needed to approve. By the time voters were asked to consider these reforms in a referendum, two-and-a-half years had passed since the agreement was signed and the momentum and enthusiasm surrounding it had subsided. When a majority of voters rejected the reforms for restructuring and modernizing government institutions, the political will to implement the changes also dwindled. In spite of this failure, international aid continued to support capacity building of government institutions, judicial reform, and civil society strengthening. And despite the setbacks, the World Bank's control of corruption index shows a significant percentage increase from 1996 to 2002—an improvement of 8.4 percent since the agreement was signed.

However, the limited political will of the government to undertake reforms seriously reduced the effects of donor assistance programs. Moreover, the 2000 presidential and legislative elections brought into power a new political party that had not signed the peace agreement and showed a limited sense of responsibility for pushing forward agreement provisions. That said, international support for fiscal policy reforms yielded some limited success: revenue collection increased in the short run due to the introduction of computerized financial control systems and mechanisms.

Overall, there is no effective institution in charge of combating corruption. Guatemala's transparency and anticorruption laws, as well as its penal code, are extremely ineffective. The government has not produced a firm national strategy or policy agenda to combat corruption, and civil society remains very weak, resulting in few opportunities to pressure government to make significant reforms. Overall, the governance and anticorruption provisions of the peace agreement can be said to have had only moderate effects on the current state of affairs.

5

Sierra Leone

The internal conflict in Sierra Leone dates to March 1991, when the rebel Revolutionary United Front of Sierra Leone (RUF/SL) was established, primarily by idealistic but unemployed and alienated young men. They received financial support, training, and resources from Liberian warlord and later president Charles Taylor. Years of political misrule and corruption were closely related to the collapse of diamond revenues from exports and the excesses of the political elite, along with a growing socioeconomic inequality between the urban wealthy and rural unemployed youth. With reduced revenues came institutional failure and drastically reduced public services. The corrupt patrimonial system harkening from independence in 1961 could no longer be tolerated.

Since diamond mining started in Sierra Leone in 1931, rampant smuggling and the corruption of public officials had become common practice, while the public benefits of the enormous diamond-generated wealth had been minimal. The country's productive sectors—agriculture, diamond and gold mining, fisheries—had been operated primarily for the benefit of the "big men" and their networks. Politics, business, government, and organized crime merged into a kleptocracy of total state capture, with the ruling elite bleeding the country of its wealth and potential.

Greed for diamond riches and, for the rebel cause, the need for diamond sales to buy arms, certainly fueled the conflict, but were not the only reasons for it. Limited mobility, reduced public service delivery, unequal access to education, and high unemployment also fed the social unrest that burst into civil war. Secretive decision-making processes, corrupt one-party rule, and a pervasive patronage system produced government mismanagement and abuses of power. World Bank and the UK Department for

International Development reports document that social discontent concerning corruption and poor governance practices were brewing for many years in Sierra Leone at local levels, as tribal chiefs abused their power, imposed illegal taxes and fees, and failed to deliver essential decentralized services and an operational customary court system. This produced uprisings as far back as 1955, and continued bad governance among chiefs was viewed as an important motivator of the RUF revolt many years later. Overall, the conflict was highlighted by excessive violence and atrocities targeted at civilians, with high levels of death and displacement and subsequent psychological and social effects.

The Negotiated Agreement

The Peace Agreement between the government of Sierra Leone and the Revolutionary United Front of Sierra Leone was signed in Lomé, Togo, on July 7, 1999. It was guided by principles of democracy, respect for human rights, good governance, and good economic management. It established an immediate cease-fire and monitoring regime, followed by a range of provisions concerning governance reforms. First, the RUF was transformed into a political party; RUF/SL members were to be appointed civil servants and serve in government, and RUF/SL leaders and members were integrated into a new unity government in leadership positions. Second, the agreement established a Commission for the Consolidation of Peace (CCP) to implement a postconflict program that ensured reconciliation and the welfare of all parties to the conflict. The CCP was given responsibility for supervising and monitoring the implementation of and compliance with the provisions of the peace agreement. Third, the agreement established a Commission for the Management of Strategic Resources, National Reconstruction and Development (CMRRD), responsible for securing and monitoring the legitimate exploitation of Sierra Leone's gold, diamonds, and other resources for the benefit of the people. The proceeds from transactions of gold and diamonds would go into the public treasury to be expended on public education, public health, infrastructure development, compensation of incapacitated war victims, and rural area priorities; the commission would operate according to principles of full transparency. Finally, Sierra Leone's current constitution would be reviewed and revised and a new national electoral commission established.

An earlier peace agreement that did not hold had been signed in Abidjan three years earlier (November 30, 1996). It dealt with good governance and anticorruption reforms in very explicit language. This failed agreement began with a commitment to promote popular participation in governance and full respect for human rights and humanitarian laws, as well as dedication to democratic development and "the maintenance of a socio-political order free of inequality, nepotism and corruption."[1] The Abidjan agreement asserted that standards of civil service accountability, integrity, and probity should be strengthened. In relation to this goal, the parties proposed establishing an office of ombudsman to promote a professional code of ethics and integrity for all public servants. It would also work to eradicate all forms of corruption. The parties agreed that judicial independence should be strengthened to ensure fair and impartial justice. This meant that selection of judges and court administration personnel should be conducted by a commission independent of the executive branch and political parties.

In addition, the Abidjan agreement called for electoral and police reforms, strengthening the police to ensure that the rule of law was upheld equally for all. Emphasis was placed on ensuring professionalism of the force and the protection of human rights. The agreement indicated that the police should avoid and combat corruption. It proposed that annual citizens' consultative conferences be conducted to encourage popular participation in government policy formulation. Finally, a quality of life section of the agreement called for improved health care, housing, educational services, clean drinking water, job creation, and protection of the environment.

The Negotiation Process

Serious peace negotiations facilitated by Côte d'Ivoire foreign minister Amara Essy led to the Abidjan Accords in late 1996. These talks began with the hope of transforming the RUF into a political party and having them participate in the upcoming presidential elections. In earlier talks in April 1996 between the government and the RUF, the two sides agreed to a ceasefire and on establishing joint working groups to develop a peace accord, disarmament, demobilization, and reintegration of combatants, as well as a plan for securing international assistance for the postagreement process. Almost immediately upon concluding these optimistic talks, the United States, United Kingdom, and European Union promised financial assistance to implement the peace. Joint working groups were established to elaborate on

---

1. "Peace Agreement between the Government of the Republic of Sierra Leone and the Revolutionary United Front of Sierra Leone," signed at Abidjan on November 30, 1996, http://www.usip.org/files/file/resources/collections/peace_agreements/sierra_leone_11301996.pdf (accessed November 15, 2010).

the points of agreement thus far. By the parties' next meeting in May, there was substantial agreement on most issues, except for power sharing as well as a repudiation of the South African mercenaries that the government had procured. This resulted in a stalemate. The Organization of African Unity (OAU) intervened to mediate and unblock the talks, which resumed in early September. After discussions between the RUF leader and the president, the government agreed to RUF demands concerning major economic, political, and social reforms, as well as a plan to transform the RUF into a political party, a general amnesty for RUF members, a promise of jobs for RUF leaders, and absorption of RUF members into the army, the police, and other government institutions. These reforms seemed to assuage RUF desires for power sharing short of immediately entering government, and amounted to major government concessions. Despite continued fighting, the two sides agreed to sign the agreement in Abidjan on November 30, 1996.

The Abidjan agreement was much more than a cease-fire and disarmament accord; it elaborated extensively on wide-ranging governance and anticorruption reforms. Unfortunately, the deal fell apart rapidly. The cease-fire never took hold and the RUF took part in a coup that overthrew the government in May 1997. There had been limited civil society participation or buy-in to the Abidjan agreements, creating a credibility gap and limited information flow to the population about the agreement. Moreover, the international community seemed to abandon the agreement soon after the talks, providing little of the proposed support that could have kept the agreement afloat.

Given the economic rewards of continuing the conflict—reportedly, the RUF and rogue army units controlled the diamond trade worth about US$250 million per year—there were few incentives to restart serious negotiations among these factions. Not until the Economic Community of West African States [Ceasefire] Monitoring Group (ECOMOG) and Nigeria announced in early 1999 that it was disengaging its peacekeepers did renewed movement for a peace agreement appear to be a viable and necessary option. This left the wealthy and armed warlords, the stakeholders with the greatest power, pulling the strings that shaped a political settlement. Another immediate stimulus for the Lomé peace negotiations in 1999 was the RUF attack on Freetown that January, which created an unprecedented number of casualties. With the failure of the government's war strategy and the pullout of peacekeepers, the government's only option was political negotiation. A May 18, 1999 cease-fire brought the two parties to the table again.

The government was unprepared for negotiations; by contrast, the RUF was very clear about its demands and vision for the country's future governance. They produced a fifty-nine-page proposal, entitled "Lasting Peace in Sierra Leone: The Revolutionary United Front (RUF-SL) Perspective and Vision," in May 1999, which demanded amnesty for RUF fighters, release of all prisoners, a power-sharing arrangement and four-year transitional government, recognition of RUF control of certain areas of the country, RUF participation in a newly formulated army, withdrawal of ECOMOG troops, and creation of an independent peacekeeping force.

The negotiations leading to the Lomé Peace Accords (signed July 7, 1999) were mediated by Togo's foreign minister, Joseph Kokou Koffigoh, and the UN secretary-general's special representative in Sierra Leone, Francis Okelo, with serious facilitation provided by the Inter-Religious Council of Sierra Leone, an NGO. A mediation committee consisting of UN, OAU, Economic Community of West African States (ECOWAS), civil society, U.S., UK, and Commonwealth representatives facilitated the sessions. The negotiations lasted for six weeks, with the mediators helping to structure the talks into three committees: military, humanitarian, and political. It was agreed quickly that substantive parts of the Abidjan Accords, in particular those dealing with human rights, humanitarian law, and a framework for civil society participation, would be carried over into the Lomé Agreement.

As suggested above, the ultimate provisions, less stringent than the Abidjan Accords in generating governance and anticorruption reforms, were crafted to appease local warlords by giving them political power in exchange for ending the violent conflict. The agreement essentially encouraged them to enjoy the spoils of office and the RUF to continue fighting after the accords were signed. However, by January 2002, disarmament of the factions was completed.

Negotiation Analysis

The prolonged and interrupted negotiation processes in Sierra Leone suggest several lessons. First, the Abidjan talks, even though they failed, gave life to new talks when the time became ripe for resolution. The Lomé negotiation picked up on some of the earlier talks' innovations and progress. Second, the rebels could demand reductions in corruption and improved governance, which were difficult for the government to reject without looking bad. However, these demands were rapidly overtaken by human greed and the desire for power, and similar charges could be leveled against the rebels. Third, mediators could serve as facilitators for the rebels, encouraging them to state their demands at the table. Fourth, international donor promises of future assistance could encourage governments to make the difficult but necessary concessions to arrive at peace agreements. Finally, power-sharing demands in peace negotiations could be vehicles to introduce good governance and anticorruption reforms.

Implementation

The peace negotiations were intended to develop an agreement on a detailed plan of action, with a schedule and specific measures to deal with governance, political, humanitarian, socioeconomic, military, and security issues. Particular institutions were slated to conduct each of the provisions, but severe levels of mistrust between the parties made implementation difficult and political will quickly dissolved. Many initial implementation problems stemmed from a lack of clarity in negotiated provisions as to how the various implementing commissions would be staffed or how each commission related to others.

By January 2002, the UN-supervised disarmament officially ended, but reforms stagnated many years into the peace implementation process. The government's commitment and capacity to address difficult governance and institutional reforms envisioned by the peace agreement was questionable. There have been some small steps toward reform, but the agreement anticipated more, and the government failed to take on more ownership of the reform process. Most governance reform efforts were sponsored by the UK, the UN Mission in Sierra Leone (UNAMSIL), the World Bank, and the International Monetary Fund, and it was their international consultants who tended to be the prime movers in implementing reforms, signaling an absence of local political will.

Regarding corruption, decentralization of services in the provinces got off to a halting start. The traditional structure of paramount chiefs in the provinces was still prevalent, drawing its power from a patronage system that had no institutionalized accountability mechanism and was prone to extensive corruption. That said, elections for district and town councils were conducted in 2004 and the first phase of decentralizing certain functions had begun. Diamond mining, too, had been widely vulnerable to patrimonial and corrupt practices and was recognized in the peace agreement as a sector sorely in need of reform. In 2003, the Kono Peace Diamond Alliance was launched to eradicate unfair practices and ensure legality, accountability, and transparency in the industry, with the help of USAID and the UK Department for International Development (DFID).

In general, the justice system was viewed as a major source of corruption and in need of a complete overhaul, but most early efforts focused only on getting the existing legal system functioning again. Donor assistance rebuilt much of the infrastructure and enabled the government to hire an adequate number of judges. But serious reforms of the entire judicial system were still needed. Access to justice in Sierra Leone had always required bribery; police, judges, and the courts were unreliable; laws were not always enforced; long delays were common; and impunity ruled. The international community—especially DFID and the World Bank—initiated studies that could serve as the foundation for action plans and strategies for more holistic reforms, but the government had only reluctantly engaged. To remedy some of these abuses, the UK government, through DFID, made a five-year commitment of US$50 million, plus technical support and grants, to initiate fundamental changes in the judicial sector. The Justice Sector Development Program, began in 2006, several years after the accords were signed.

Early and more far-reaching judicial reforms were anticipated by the peace agreement but lagged behind in implementation. Part of the problem was that provisions relating to judicial reform and the rule of law lacked sufficient detail and the needed personnel and infrastructure were not available. Typically, it is difficult for warring parties to discuss or address such issues immediately after a civil war ends, unless there is serious international involvement and pressure. Without such pressure, local political will, or clearly defined negotiated provisions, issues pertaining to accountability, impunity, truth-seeking, and related matters of justice have to be dealt with in later postagreement negotiations.

An anticorruption commission was established in 2000 with both investigatory and prosecutorial powers. However, the commission was overpoliticized and lacked sufficient independence to be effective. Cases passed to the attorney general for prosecution were plagued by insufficient documentation. Few have led to court cases and most indictments have dealt only with petty corruption cases, not larger and more serious grand corruption scandals. Advocacy groups and media coverage that can maintain pressure on government to pursue such cases have been sorely lacking.

Sierra Leone's Special Court and Truth and Reconciliation Commission (TRC) were established to promote accountability and reconciliation, respectively. The court began operations in 2002 and issued several indictments at a rather aggressive pace. The TRC also got underway in 2002, but suffered from funding shortages and apparent lack of interest from the government and populace.

In particular, some of the major postagreement donor assistance programs are summarized below:[2]

- **Anticorruption institutions.** Support was provided to establish the Anticorruption Commission to investigate instances of alleged or suspected corruption as well as to educate, enlist, and foster public support in the fight against corruption. The program also supported an anticorruption strategy to disseminate information and promote public support via media campaigns and educational materials for youth focus groups; sponsored by DFID, World Bank, GTZ, and UNDP between 2005 and 2008.

- **Local governance support.** A Governance Reform Secretariat was developed and a code of ethics for the private sector was approved; sponsored by the Government of Sierra Leone.

- **Audit and control.** A public expenditure tracking survey (PETS) was supported to track budgetary expenditures in state agencies and increase transparency through capacity building and training. As well, the Auditor General's Department (AGD) was supported; sponsored by the UNDP and EU in 2001.

- **Public financial management.** The Economic Rehabilitation and Economic Management Program promoted good governance through institutional capacity building, financial management systems, and supporting the rule of law; sponsored by DFID.

- **Civil society initiatives.** Support for West African Civil Society Networks (in Guinea, Liberia, and Sierra Leone) was provided to strengthen effective use of the internet and community radio; sponsored by USAID through the Leland Initiative, 2005 to 2007.

- **Media and public awareness programs.** The Media Development Project supported the establishment of an independent media commission. It provided capacity building and technical support for

2. Awareness Times, "UNDP Supports Ministry Of Finance and Economic Development to Enhance Transparency, Accountability and Participation (CAP) in The National Budget Process in Sierra Leone," February 8, 2008, http://news.sl/drwebsite/publish/article_20057619.shtml (accessed December 7, 2010); Joel Cutting and Gladwell Otieno, "Annual Review 2006 of DFID Support to Anticorruption Commission Phase 2 in Sierra Leone," Department for International Development, UK, January 25, 2007; Chris Mahoney, "Addressing Corruption in Post-Conflict Sierra Leone," Anticorruption Commission, Republic of Sierra Leone, http://www.anticorruption.sl/addressing_corruption. htm (accessed December 7, 2010); USAID, "Peace Diamond Alliance Helps Mining Communities in Sierra Leone," Sub-Saharan Africa Success Stories, http://africastories.usaid.gov/search_details.cfm? storyID=210&countryID=22&sectorID=0&yearID=4 (accessed December 7, 2010).

independent radio, television, the Sierra Leone News Agency (SLENA), and public and privately-owned newspapers; sponsored by the Thomson Foundation (UK) from 2000 to 2003.

- **Private sector reforms.** Programs were instituted to monitor diamond royalties and fees, inform miners of the value of stones, and create public awareness of diamond mining issues. These efforts supported anticorruption measures, the introduction of standards into the diamond industry, and advice on diamond dealing and exporting. The Peace Diamond Alliance (2002–06) and a study to develop a strategy for the management of diamond-producing areas in Sierra Leone were sponsored by USAID, DFID, and Amco Robertson Mineral Services (ARMS).

Conclusions

The Sierra Leone peace agreement received international support to establish an anticorruption commission, restore rule of law, and assist in managing the diamond industry. However, limited local political will and inconsistent international support has yielded mixed results. The World Bank control of corruption index shows a positive trend, though with small improvements (1.4 percent), over the five years since the peace agreement was signed.

The Anticorruption Act and several other laws and institutions aimed at ensuring sustainable democratic good governance have supported local efforts to fight corruption, and overall, Sierra Leone has progressed in criminalizing corrupt practices. But the country lacks sufficient mechanisms to ensure a predictable rule of law. The police force had been one of the most corrupted institutions and currently still lacks the resources and competencies to uphold the rule of law. In other sectors, under the Economic Rehabilitation and Recovery Credit, the government has utilized an effective fiscal and expenditure control policy to minimize corruption and eradicate nontransparent budgetary transactions. The European Union has supported the establishment of a financial information system in the auditor general's department. USAID has achieved a degree of success in the diamond mining sector, which used to be one of the country's most corrupt industries. The creation and mobilization of the Peace Diamond Alliance has educated workers about their rights and created a mechanism to monitor diamond royalties and fees. As a result, revenue collection from the diamond industry has increased and significant amounts are returned to local communities to benefit public service delivery.

6

Burundi

Burundi experienced four decades of civil strife between the dominant Tutsi minority and the Hutu majority from the time of its independence in 1961. Civil war broke out in earnest in 1993, a few months after the first democratic elections selected a Hutu president and Hutu-led parliament. The president was assassinated shortly after and, until the peace agreement was signed, an estimated 400,000 people were killed. Over 800,000 fled the country.

The list of grievances that catalyzed the violence is long, including political exclusion based on ethnicity—the military, judiciary, educational system, business sector, and mass media were traditionally dominated by the minority Tutsi—and the deprivation of rights based on ethnicity, clan, region, and class. Economic and political powers were concentrated in the urban elite and there were also conflicts over access to land. Given these problems, it is easy to see how a culture of corruption and impunity was widespread. There was no judicial impartiality or legal accountability. The courts were corrupt, failed governance institutions were scarred by nepotism, the military held political dominance and impunity, and a skewed economic development strategy was based on regional favoritism.

The Negotiated Agreement

The Arusha Agreement, signed on August 28, 2000, outlines a wide range of anticorruption principles meant to help Burundi govern itself under a new constitution after transition. They range from constitutional provisions that outline the values of transparency and accountability in government to more specific measures relating to public administration, education, justice, and the economy. The agreement explicitly references issues of corruption control, oversight, and openness across many governance domains.[1]

Protocol 1 of the agreement contains several measures to resolve governance problems, all to be framed within a new constitution written to promote the values of justice, the rule of law, democracy, and good governance, among others. Article 7 of the agreement calls for "a transparent administration committed to the sound management of public affairs." Other provisions in Protocol 1 call for the depoliticization and transparency of competitive entrance examinations into the civil service. In the education sector, Protocol 1 provisions call for "transparency and fairness in non-competitive and competitive examinations." In the judicial sector, the agreement calls for "impartial and independent justice," reforms to the criminal and civil codes and the criminal procedures code, reform of the judicial service commission to ensure judicial independence, and establishment of an ombudsperson's office to oversee citizen rights. For the economy, the agreement specifically calls for "legislation and structures for combating financial crime and corruption (tax legislation, customs legislation, legislation on public markets, etc.), and recovery of State property plundered by some citizens."

Protocol 2 establishes a wide range of democracy and good governance principles and values to guide the transitional peace process and beyond. Fundamental values include a government that is accountable to the people, based on the rule of law and the principles of good governance and transparency in the management of public affairs. Political party financing laws are to be designed to ensure transparency in the functioning of parties and electoral campaigns, and an elections commission established to guarantee independence in the electoral process. The national assembly is to oversee the actions of government and a court of audit that reports to the assembly is to examine and certify that public funds are used appropriately. The senate is to appoint or confirm members of the judiciary and the prosecutor, and the ombudsperson is to ensure their independence from the executive. The president and local government executives may be impeached for misconduct, corruption, or embezzlement, and civil servants found and convicted of corruption of all kinds are to be dismissed and punished according to the law. To ensure that these reforms are implemented, the agreement provides for a commission of the transitional national assembly to oversee the reforms in public and justice administration. In addition, the transitional government was directed to implement the following reforms:

---

1. The appendix contains the actual anticorruption and good governance provisions from the negotiated agreements.

Steps shall be taken to discourage corruption, to denounce officials guilty of corruption, to enforce all legislation related to corruption, to establish effective oversight bodies, to improve working conditions in the judicial sector and to take necessary measures to require civil servants to report instances of corruption;

The necessary measures shall be taken ... to deal with the problem of impunity and take any other steps required to ensure that any travesties of justice are dealt with or re-opened (from Protocol 2, Article 17).

The Negotiation Process

How and why did the peace negotiation for Burundi produce explicit anticorruption provisions? From April 1996 until his death in 1999, Julius Nyerere, the former Tanzanian president, facilitated and mediated the talks that led to the Arusha Agreement. Nelson Mandela succeeded Nyerere in December 1999 and brought the negotiations to their ultimate agreement. The talks were initiated to deal explicitly with the long history of escalating civil war between the Hutu majority and the Tutsi minority, stimulated by the large number of extremist groups on both sides. Many saw Nyerere as the only one who could gain the confidence of the various groups, although there were suspicions about his evenhandedness among Tutsis because he had supported Hutu interests for majority rule. In addition to the local Burundian parties, country leaders from the Great Lakes region were also included in the negotiations.

The initial meetings in 1996 brought together representatives of thirteen political parties, but gradually smaller parties were invited to make the talks more inclusive. These early sessions included discussions of introducing regional peacekeeping forces to stop the killing and create a semblance of stability. Also discussed was the possibility of imposing a trade blockade on Burundi to pressure the government to a cease-fire and push the ruling Tutsis into serious negotiations. These trade sanctions were established and, as a result, the government withdrew from the talks for two years in protest. Only in June 1998 did the government agree to reengage with the peace process in Arusha. Nineteen Burundian delegations participated, with seventeen representing political parties, one the government, and one the national assembly. In addition, to demonstrate the gravity of the talks, the presidents of Kenya, Uganda, Rwanda, and Tanzania participated, as did the prime ministers of Ethiopia and Zaire.

Nyerere promoted inclusivity as a basic principle especially in the 1998 negotiations, seeking to involve all parties to the conflict, as participation by only the two major political parties would not suffice to reach and sustain a peace agreement. Even secondary parties were included: women's and religious groups, regional states to serve as guarantors of the ultimate agreement, and international donors. However, Nyerere failed to bring in the extremist rebel groups, despite continued attempts. Several groups splintered and all wanted seats at the table, producing additional within-group bickering and deadlock. In the end, Nyerere chose to recognize the existing leaders and exclude the rebels, who continued to remain at war with the government, seeking to spoil the agreement.

The 1998 resumption of negotiations was supported by US$15 million provided by Western donors; the European Union gave the most resources to the negotiation process itself. These funds facilitated extensive pre-negotiation and informal consultations by Nyerere and his associates with the various factions to develop the issue structure and organizational framework of the upcoming talks.

Nyerere designed a detailed committee structure to address the many complex issues at hand and develop ownership of the final agreement by the large number of negotiation participants. This approach dovetailed with Nyerere's belief in local self-reliance. Five issue-focused committees were established to guide the work of the negotiations on the nature of the conflict and solutions, strategies for democracy and good governance, strategies for peace and security, economic reconstruction and development, and implementing the agreement. Each committee included representatives from all the Burundian delegations, plus a chair and vice-chair (to serve as mediators) and resource experts.

Committee 2, dealing with future democracy and governance practices, was divided into seven working groups: political parties, legislature, executive, judiciary, electoral system, administration, and transitional arrangements. As with all the other committees, in the end, there was no conclusive agreement on all issues or subissues. The analytical and intellectual approach of the committee system sought to deal with all problems all at once, and this proved to be slow and cumbersome. As the approach operated on consensus, it was difficult to reach agreement on delicate issues. The local delegations had formed coalitions based on ethnicity; Hutus formed the Group of Seven and Tutsis the Group of Ten. The consensus approach sought to get parties to talk with one another and build mutual confidence and trust, yielding a path toward compromise, but it did not work well.

When Mandela took over as facilitator of the talks in late 1999, he wanted to include the breakaway rebel groups in the negotiations, but he too failed.

He succeeded, however, in including more international leaders in the process which generated greater legitimacy, backing, and resources for the negotiations, putting greater pressure on the Burundian government. Mandela's major contribution to the negotiation structure that Nyerere established was to introduce a mechanism of "sufficient consensus." With this approach, vetoes by smaller groups in the committee system could be avoided. If there were disagreements in the committees, the problems would be referred to smaller groups for solution. He also imposed a deadline of August 28, 2000 for a signed agreement. Thirteen of the nineteen delegations signed on that date. The remaining six Tutsi holdouts finally signed on September 20. An implementing monitoring committee was created, but an essential cease-fire was not signed because rebel groups remained outside the agreement.

At a donor conference held in December 2000, Mandela confirmed that the peace agreement signed in August was not an end in itself, but only the beginning of the reconstruction. Postagreement negotiations were required for unresolved issues, especially signing on to the cease-fire. The transitional government continued to work at getting rebel factions to agree to the principles of Arusha, and by late 2002, three new groups signed the cease-fire agreement. In 2003, 2005, and 2006, additional rebel groups signed on, but the cease-fires failed to hold. The rebels had not been exposed to the dialogue and compromise of the negotiation process as had the core delegations; they were asked to accept a fait accompli, which they ultimately did, but they did not feel obligated to fulfill its mandate. Rebel groups then were offered ministry positions and integrated into the national defense forces, and regional countries continued to attempt to broker cease-fires and threaten the government with sanctions, but with halting successes and failures.

Meanwhile, the transitional government continued to push ahead with implementing other provisions of the Arusha agreement. The transfer of the shared presidency was accomplished in April 2003 and the constitutional referendum was conducted successfully in March 2005. By late 2007, international commentators agreed that Burundi had made substantial progress in developing democratic practices and easing interethnic tensions. One rebel group, the Party for the Liberation of the Hutu People (PALIPEHUTU-FNL), which is strong in the western provinces, was the last holdout from the cease-fire, threatening the fragile situation until agreeing to lay down arms in May 2008.

The focus on corruption and good governance issues within the negotiation process was both internally and externally driven. From 1987 to 1993, Burundi experimented in political and economic reforms, as well as a constitutional review process under President Pierre Buyoya. Political and pluralistic changes resulting from these reforms produced the election of the first Hutu president in 1993, who was assassinated shortly thereafter. With a fall into further violence, the democratic experiment quickly ended, but with a call for external intervention to end the instability in the form of an OAU military mission.

By May 1994, UN-mediated negotiations began to promote internal power sharing, yielding the Convention on Government in September 1994. This agreement created a short-lived national security council that curbed presidential power and spurred debate on the ethnic composition of the judiciary, army, and administration. In part, because the army had veto power within this council, most initiatives ended in stalemate and instability. By 1995, regional presidents invited former U.S. president Jimmy Carter to intervene to bring peace and security to the Great Lakes region. Through a series of conferences, he restarted discussions—this time with the active participation of regional delegations—about refugee repatriation, cross-border raids, arms trafficking, the constitution, and the army's mission. One of the forward-looking decisions of these conferences was the appointment of Julius Nyerere as the principal mediator to find a solution to power sharing in Burundi.

When Nyerere's initial facilitation in 1996 failed, he moved quickly to build regional support for economic sanctions against the Burundi government, hoping to pressure the regime to restart negotiations. But by 1998, a UN report concluded that sanctions had not only failed to restart serious talks, but had blocked trade and complicated humanitarian work; several regional and other interested governments also had lost faith in the sanctions and in Nyerere's leadership of the mediation efforts.

Western donors and governments and international organizations that had been supporting the mediation efforts sought to get Nyerere to restart the negotiations using a different tack. At the June 1998 Arusha meeting, a three-tiered strategy was developed: There would be informal mediator-party consultations, five committees would be established to work out solutions on key agenda issues, and plenary sessions would be held to make ultimate decisions. Moving ahead with the negotiation framework was to be predicated on achieving a cease-fire; while it did not hold from the very beginning, the process laid out in the framework moved ahead anyway.

The committee concept was the key feature that catalyzed negotiation of corruption and governance issues. The idea was to disentangle the issues on which the parties disagreed, build confidence, and develop communication channels by breaking down complex issues into simpler subissues, enabling trade-offs. All parties were initially represented on each of the five commit-tees. In addition, each committee was chaired by an international personality, at the instigation of the Western sponsors who sought to improve the quality of the mediation efforts and reduce any perceived bias that Nyerere and his Tanzanian staff introduced; Nyerere's association with the sanctions regime was seen by some to stymie negotiation progress. The Western sponsors be-lieved that the five committee chairs would introduce new leadership and a buffer with Nyerere.

However, by January 1999, the committees had made little progress. With eighteen negotiators in each committee, there was much democracy, but minimal responsibility from the parties to achieve results. Many of the Western sponsors and regional governments blamed the laxity of manage-ment procedures, the absence of strict deadlines, and the large number of parties within the negotiations for the failure of the committee system. In addition, some blamed the generous daily per diem that donors provided to all negotiating party representatives as another factor in prolonging the negotiation process. In May 1999, the Hutu parties met independently to develop a common negotiating position and formed the Group of Seven. In response, the Tutsi parties quickly established their coalition. The govern-ment, the Tutsi-dominated Union for National Progress (UPRONA), and the national assembly formed the Partnership Group. This consolidation of actors, in fact, enhanced the efficiency of the negotiations.

Negotiation Analysis

Nyerere emphasized a political, over a military, solution to the conflict in Burundi. To accomplish this, he paid special attention to breaking the nego-tiation process into committees and working groups to develop a systematic, comprehensive, and rather detailed agreement incorporating extensive con-sideration of governance and anticorruption measures. He wanted to develop a positive vision of the future for Burundians to implement, and he sought to involve all parties in this vision so they would have local ownership.

The process ultimately was useful in achieving Nyerere's objective, but it suffered from several flaws. First, it did not pay sufficient attention to achiev-ing a successful and sustainable cease-fire as a prerequisite for following up with political provisions. As a result, many, though not all, of the politi-cal measures were delayed or not implemented. Second, all parties were not included in the negotiation process from the beginning. While many were eventually brought into the process later on, they did not experience true and sincere buy-in to the agreement's provisions; the parties not originally included were factions or splinter groups of included parties and tended to represent the more belligerent elements. Those already at the table had insisted on excluding them as new and separate delegations to the peace process. But by excluding them, they guaranteed their role as spoilers of the agreement early in the process. Third, the consensus rule in the negotiation committees became unworkable because of the large number of parties and interests that needed to be served, and the long time it took to reach agreement as a result. International donors especially lost patience with the process. As a result, alternate approaches—coalition-building and softer consensus rules—were introduced. Finally, civil society groups were excluded from the peace process. They primarily represented elite Tutsi interests and Hutu political parties strongly opposed them.

Implementation

Despite the large number of signatories to the 2000 Arusha agreement, some major Hutu rebel groups did not participate in the peace process at all and did not lay down their arms when the cease-fire was agreed to. According to the International Crisis Group in 2002:

> The Arusha accord, which was obtained under pressure from the region and the international community, is not sufficient. Although it was supposed to be the Bible of the Burundian peace process, it is only the Old Testament. An entire book on negotiations remains to be written and as long as stakes are high and fears prevail in the parties' minds, this endeavor will require patience, competence and perseverance. The South African facilitation team needs to understand that it will have to lead the lion share of the peace process: negotiating an end to the war. It also has to negotiate individual and collective security interests, which are probably the most difficult issues in the Burundian conflict.[2]

What still needed attention were postagreement negotiations on cease-fires with rebel groups that were not parties to the Arusha negotiations. These groups were very real spoilers: The violence had not stopped when the agreement was signed and donors were reluctant to support the postagreement implementation process until there was relative security and stabilization.

By November 2003, a cease-fire agreement and power-sharing protocol was reached with the largest of these outlier groups, the National Council for the Defense of Democracy-Forces for the Defense of Democracy (CNDD-FDD). The PALIPEHUTU-FNL, the last active rebel group,

---

2. International Crisis Group, "Burundi after Six Months of Transition: Continuing the War or Winning Peace?" *Africa Report* no. 46, International Crisis Group, Brussels, May 24, 2002, 20–21.

signed a cease-fire agreement in September 2006, but it was not successfully implemented. As an outlier to the process, this armed wing which was especially strong in the countryside and the western provinces spread fear that fighting would resume. In April 2008, the PALIPEHUTU-FNL's spoiler tendencies emerged again when violence escalated and the rebel group attacked Burundian government military positions in contravention of the September agreement. However, by late May 2008, a lasting cease-fire with the PALIPEHUTU-FNL was signed, mediated by South Africa. It resolved outstanding issues, primarily related to integrating the rebels into the security forces and political institutions. Finally, in April 2009, this armed wing laid down its arms and officially transformed itself into a political party in a ceremony supervised by the African Union.

The 2000 agreement provided for a three-year implementation period to restore state institutions and the rule of law. This was extended to August 2005, which gave the parties time to hold elections, demobilize combatants, hold a referendum to ratify a new constitution and promulgate the new document. The former Hutu rebels (CNDD-FDD) clearly won the 2005 elections at the national and local levels, taking a majority of seats in parliament and communal councils. As the first democratically elected government since 1993, the CNDD-FDD was faced with reconstructing the economy, building government institutions, and responding to continuing security problems, all of which were part of implementing the peace agreements. However, the government's initial response to these challenges was to disregard the rule of law, leading to a rise in corruption. With limited accountability, opposition politicians were arrested on questionable charges, there was political interference in public procurements, and state-owned enterprises were restaffed, resulting in charges of favoritism and patronage. Moreover, the government clamped down on press and associational freedoms. As a result, the European Union and the World Bank suspended their budgetary assistance pending an audit.

Because of the corruption problems, disbursement of international assistance was slow. In 2006, the United Nations established a peacebuilding commission for Burundi to bring together current and future donors—the World Bank, European Union, African Union, UN specialized agencies, bilateral donors, and NGOs—with the government. The commission could pressure the government to make progress on crucial governance and human rights priorities.

With donor assistance, key anticorruption institutions have been established, but they have not been protected from political interference and have very little power to execute their mandates. Similarly, some laws—such as an antimoney laundering law and an electoral code of conduct—were adopted but not put into practice. Donor programs to support civil service reform at the central and community levels were conducted, but there is still a pervasive culture of corruption among civil servants. In tax collections and customs duties, cheating is rampant and civil servants tend to turn a blind eye.

Postwar judicial reform has faced many challenges, including restoration of the rule of law, impunity for crimes, and embedded corruption in the judicial apparatus and public services. There is a general public perception that impunity is rampant and judicial decisions are not enforced. The popular view is that corruption cases have focused primarily on the small fish, while the big players are not touched. Courts are generally reluctant to publish their decisions. Pervasive ethnic divisions in the judiciary—one of the causes of the conflict—persist.

The international community has worked with the Burundian justice system since the 2000 peace agreement to implement the reforms envisioned in that document. In general, donor support for judicial reforms has had mixed results in different provinces due to coordination problems across actors and differences in focus across geographic regions. Many projects have been initiated in line with the provisions of the negotiated agreement to strengthen the justice system, including training of judges, judicial staff, and police officers; improvements in working conditions; reediting, harmonization, and translation of legislation; greater access to justice for the population; technical assistance to lawyers and support to the Bar Association; reforms to jails and prisons; assistance to the new civilian police force; advocacy for reforms to fight against impunity and corruption; and reforms to the land laws. On the negative side, the potential for mutually supportive cooperation between the formal justice system and the traditional system for resolving conflicts has not been tapped effectively. Some international donor assistance has focused on reinvigorating and developing the capacity of the traditional justice system, but it has not been sufficient. There are also important gaps in donor efforts, including the fight against impunity and addressing land issues.

In general, there is a lack of political will and government commitment to work in the judicial sector to ensure that real change is implemented. Overall, the percentage of the national budget devoted to the judicial system is viewed as insufficient, as is international financial support provided to this sector.

Brief highlights of postagreement donor assistance programs include:[3]

- **Anticorruption institutions.** Programs have provided technical assistance to increase the capacity of key anticorruption institutions. Civic institutions were trained in corruption reporting and investigation techniques. Activities also included an in-depth, in-country governance and anticorruption diagnostics survey to assist the government in policy design toward improving governance and reducing corruption; support provided by IFES, World Bank, the Ministry of Good Governance, and Burundian Steering Committee comprising members of civil society organizations from 2006 to 2007.
- **Local governance support.** Programs have trained over 4,400 political and military elite in interest-based negotiations, communications, mediation, conflict analysis, strategic planning, and management; the Burundi Leadership Training Program was sponsored by USAID, the World Bank, and the Woodrow Wilson Center, 2002–05.
- **Service delivery reform.** The Community and Social Development Project (2007–12) established a decentralized, participatory, and transparent financing mechanism that empowers local governments and communities to provide better and more equitable local service delivery. The program supported community empowerment, capacity building (planning, managerial, financial, and technical), socioeconomic projects, and social cohesion activities; sponsored by the World Bank.
- **Judicial reform.** Support programs have reconstructed the judicial system of Burundi by providing assistance to enhance the functions of the Supreme Court, draft national laws and regulations, and promote the judicial newspaper to disseminate new laws and regulations. The

---

3. Tracy Dexter and Philippe Ntahombaye, *The Role of Informal Justice Systems in Fostering the Rule of Law in Post-Conflict Situations: The Case of Burundi* (Geneva: Centre for Humanitarian Dialogue, 2005); Howard Wolpe and Steve McDonald, "Burundi's Transition: Training Leaders for Peace," *Journal of Democracy* 17, no. 1 (January 2006): 132–38; Howard Wolpe, Steve Mcdonald, Eugene Nindorera, Elizabeth McClintock, Alain Lempereur, Fabien Nsengimana, Nicole Rumeau, and Alli Blair, "Rebuilding Peace and State Capacity in War-torn Burundi," *The Round Table* 93, no. 375 (July 2004): 457–467; World Bank Institute, "Burundi Governance Diagnostic," http://web.worldbank.org/WBSITE/EXTERNAL/WBI/EXTWBIGOVANTCOR/0,,contentMDK:21402604~pagePK:64168445~piPK:64168309~theSitePK:1740530,00.html (accessed December 7, 2010); USAID, "USAID Burundi Annual Report 2005," http://pdf.usaid.gov/pdf_docs/Pdacd858.pdf (accessed December 7, 2010); World Bank, "Burundi," http://siteresources.worldbank.org/CDFINTRANET/Overview/21192569/BurundiFINALDecember312006.doc (accessed December 7, 2010); International Foundation for Electoral Systems, "Burundi," http://www.ifes.org/burundi.html (accessed December 7, 2010); Internal UN Peacebuilding Support Office (PBSO), "Mapping External Resource Flows to Burundi," PBSO paper, March, 10, 2007, http://www.un.org/peace/peacebuilding/Country-Specific%20Configurations/Burundi/Mapping%20resource%20flows%20Burundi.pdf (accessed December 7, 2010).

programs also supported civil society involvement in the judicial development process; sponsored by GTZ (Germany), Ministry of Justice, Supreme Court, State Public Prosecutor, National Legislation Commission, and the Supreme Council of Justice (Conseil supérieur de la magistrature) from 2003 to 2007.

- **Media and public awareness programs.** Programs have strengthened the mass media during the transition to advocate for effective government, rule of law, and conflict mitigation; sponsored by USAID from 2003 to 2005.

Conclusions

The Burundi agreement of 2000 was one of the most detailed good governance and anticorruption-oriented peace agreements to date. However, statebuilding processes have moved slowly, due in part to ongoing rebel attacks. Despite this, some improvement in the World Bank Institute's control of corruption indicator is evident. Over a five-year period after the agreement was signed, Burundi registered a change on the indicator scale of 4.2 percent, a small but meaningful advance in the index.

Following the peace agreement, international donor assistance was directed to increase the capacity of government institutions and political leadership. Capacity-building training efforts were conducted from the office of the president to the grassroots. Burundi successfully updated its constitution, creating strong laws and institutions to fight corruption, at least on paper; and a good governance ministry, a corruption court with a prosecutor, a specialized police squad against corruption, a state general inspection service, and a specific law against corruption were adopted. However, a lack of political will and professional resources hindered the government's ability to put these laws and institutions into full practice and reduced the public's accessibility to relevant agencies.

Judicial reform and strengthening the rule of law were major challenges for Burundi and the international donor community, and development in this sector has shown mixed results. International aid was targeted at legislative drafting, code harmonization to international standards, and capacity building in the courts and among judges and lawyers to practice the rule of law. However, real change in this sector was still subject to political manipulation and bribery. Perhaps most important, Burundi developed no effective oversight bodies to control and manage the judicial and financial development of the country. No effective ombudsman was established in practice. On the other hand, judicial accountability has been slowly taking form through publicized court verdicts and public accessibility to judicial reports. Donor assistance programs have sought actively to involve civil society into the policy and legislative development process. In addition, the media is beginning to report on and investigate corruption cases. Overall, the effect of Burundi's integrity-infused peace agreement can be viewed as just barely successful to date.

7

Papua New Guinea

Bougainville's secessionist conflict from Papua New Guinea (PNG) began in 1989 as an indigenous protest against the Australian-owned copper mining firm that provided a large percentage of PNG's tax revenue base. Bougainvilleans felt they were paying for more than their fair share of the overall country's development, while suffering loss of land ownership, inequitable treatment of local workers, and environmental damage. Grievances extended to accusations of bribery and corruption among PNG officials over the distribution of mine revenues. Moreover, the lack of provincial autonomy and political participation led to charges of unaccountable governance. Bougainvilleans wanted more fiscal and political self-reliance, which Papua New Guinea denied them. The PNG government sought to maintain its dealings with mining interests behind closed doors.

Violent clashes spread between the PNG defense forces and the Bougainville Revolutionary Army (BRA). The government army was given the task of suppressing the rebellion, which they undertook with extreme brutality and lack of discipline. By 1990, a cease-fire was declared and Papua New Guinea decided to withdraw all forces from the island; the BRA was in control. Papua New Guinea then declared a blockade of Bougainville and BRA declared the Independent Republic of Bougainville in May 1990. Thousands died for lack of medical supplies, and anarchy and conflict spread, with Papua New Guinea providing arms to resistance forces, and the PNG defense forces fostering attacks against the Bougainvilleans. Attempts to start negotiations in 1994 to end the conflict, with United Nations observers and an Australian peacekeeping force, were fruitless. By 1997, PNG resorted to hiring British mercenaries to take back the secessionist island. The conflict was resolved through a negotiated cease-fire in 1997 and a subsequent comprehensive peace agreement in 2001. During that time, 15,000 people died and about one-third of the population of 200,000 was displaced.

The Negotiated Agreement

The Bougainville Peace Agreement, signed at Arawa on August 30, 2001, consisted of three major elements: a deferred referendum for Bougainvilleans on independence from Papua New Guinea, a high degree of autonomy for Bougainville that would be guaranteed by changes to the PNG constitution, and a plan to disarm ex-combatants.

It also affirmed many good governance and anticorruption objectives to be achieved in the postagreement period. In addition to calling for an immediate cease-fire, the agreement provided for "a democratic and accountable system of government for Bougainville that meets internationally accepted standards of good governance, including protection of human rights."[1] It established Bougainville as an autonomous region within Papua New Guinea, with its own constitution and accountable institutions and procedures.

In addition to featuring the establishment of a local judiciary in the autonomous region, the agreement focused in detail on issues related to the accountability of public expenditures. A public accounts committee would be created in the legislature and regular audits performed of provincial accounts and revenues in the autonomous Bougainville government. Grants provided to Bougainville also would be subject to audit by the auditor-general established under the national constitution. If audits disclosed systematic and widespread abuse or misuse of funds, remedies would be implemented in consultation with the national government.

The Negotiation Process

Early but failed peace conferences in 1994 and afterward helped to develop personal relationships among key stakeholders on all sides. The 1997 Burnham Truce and the Lincoln Agreement that followed in 1998 ended the conflict with a cease-fire that experienced no major violations. The negotiations for those agreements recognized that political issues could be addressed only with the violence ended and security established. As a result, the BRA and interim government accepted these as limited objectives for the talks. The agreements established a truce and cease-fire, a neutral body to

1. Bougainville Peace Agreement, paragraph B, http://www.c-r.org/our-work/accord/png-bougainville/key-texts37.php (accessed November 15, 2010).

monitor the cease-fire, and a body representing the two major protagonists to which the cease-fire monitors would report. Regional countries contributed to the monitoring forces, as did the United Nations Observer Mission in Bougainville (UNOMB). Implementing these provisions had immediate and positive effects. Fighting ceased, freedom of movement was renewed, refugee camps were closed, people returned to their villages, and basic government delivery of health and education services began again.

After the first phase of talks, further negotiations dealt with security, confidence building, and arrangements for a proposed Bougainville Reconciliation Government. Radical and moderate factions in Bougainville differed on many positions, slowing the talks. However, in the last two years of negotiations, the remaining political issues that divided the internal parties were resolved. These talks were guided by a 1999 position paper developed by the Bougainville People's Congress, which served as a negotiating agenda. This involved extensive compromises among the moderate and radical factions on issues of independence, elections, and autonomy. The paper, entitled "Options for Negotiations on a Political Solution: A Framework for Evaluation," laid out nine broad options for a future political settlement, from immediate independence to acceptance of a new provincial government system within Papua New Guinea.[2] For each of these options, the paper elaborated on the main issues and requirements that would need to be satisfied in future negotiations. Interests and positions on each issue were carefully analyzed to ensure that each faction's concerns were addressed. Options were rated and then discussed extensively across regions. In the end, a specific Bougainville negotiation position was adopted—a deferred and binding referendum on independence and the highest possible autonomy in the interim—that guided the negotiations to follow. It was agreed that these two issues should be dealt with as a single indivisible package.

The PNG government publicly opposed independence and ruled out the possibility of a referendum. The national government's position was to maintain peace by promoting several issues: weapons disposal; restoration of governance functions and civil authority through the police, courts, and prisons; and restoration of reliable public services. If these features were established at this stage, then at a later stage, negotiations could resume to consider a joint search for mutually acceptable political outcomes concerning greater autonomy.

---

2. Anthony J. Regan, "Resolving Two Dimensions of Conflict: The Dynamics of Consent, Consensus, and Compromise," *Accord* 12 (2002), available at http://www.c-r.org/our-work/accord/png-bougainville/resolving.php (accessed December 7, 2010).

In the negotiations themselves, the Bougainville position was stated clearly and immediately overpowered the national government's position. The Bougainvilleans believed that the PNG negotiation approach was meant to generate a long and drawn-out process that would lower the expectations of radical independence seekers. They also believed that the international community was poised to apply pressure for more moderate options. At the table, they adopted a clear strategy that tied together the large number of factions that were participating. All factions were included in negotiating teams, even though this resulted in large and unwieldy groups. At the same time, the Bougainvilleans agreed to speak with a single unified voice. Another aspect of the strategy was to regularly remind the PNG delegation that a failed negotiation process could lead to the ascendancy of more radical secessionist factions and a return to violence.

After one year of talks largely focused on the referendum issue, a formula was developed to eventually hold the referendum, but not for at least ten years, and to impose some requirements favored by the PNG government related to good governance and weapons disposal. While these provisions had been proposed earlier and then rejected, they were eventually agreed as a result of a shuttle mediation effort by the Australian minister of foreign affairs and trade, the replacement of a key PNG minister, and the imminent deadline of a PNG parliamentary election the following year. With the referendum issue resolved, the negotiations moved on to weapons disposal and autonomy, the latter including options related to governance, corruption, transparency, and accountability. These institutional and governance issues turned out to be sticking points that were resolved during the final five weeks of nonstop negotiation. In the end, Bougainville was given the right within Papua New Guinea to develop its own constitution and institutions, requiring that they adhere to basic standards of good governance and accountability.

Negotiation Analysis

What features of the negotiation process were essential to pushing the talks forward to the peace agreement? One positive element was the early leadership of the premier of the Bougainville transitional government, Theodore Miriung, who engaged in early talks with the PNG government and was a proponent of building bridges between all Bougainville factions. After his assassination in 1996, other leaders continued his efforts. Observers say that including all factions, led primarily by those in the center, was a key to progress in the talks. The time it took to negotiate all the issues on the agenda was also seen as a positive feature. Over the many negotiating sessions that took place, each side learned a lot about the interests, difficulties, and reasoning of the other side, producing a sense of empathy and cooperation.

Both sides made major compromises; the final agreement left open the possibility of secession in the longer term. But the Bougainvilleans also conceded on conditions for the referendum and autonomy. Indigenous reconciliation practices were crucial to resolving the conflict, especially given the large number of factions involved, and the cultural norm of balanced reciprocity in Bougainvillean traditional society helped to sow the seeds for compromises made by all parties. The international community played a significant part as well, through discrete interventions and mediation efforts, and by providing a secure environment through its monitoring forces. Other countries assumed a facilitative and nondominating role, allowing for local control and ownership of the process.

Implementation

Since the signing of the peace agreement in 2001, implementation has proceeded slowly but positively, with high levels of cooperation between Bougainville groups and the PNG government. PNG military forces began to withdraw from Bougainville in 2001. Weapons disposal started immediately and ended in 2005 with a high level of success. The constitutional changes needed to implement the accords were drafted jointly and adopted by the PNG legislature in 2002. Constitutional provisions for the Bougainville autonomous government were developed in a participatory fashion and elections conducted, allowing the Bougainville government to begin operation in June 2005.

Postagreement donor assistance programs meant to support provisions in the peace agreement include the following activities, among many others:[3]

---

3. AusAID, "Papua New Guinea: Annual Program Performance Update 2007," http://www.ausaid.gov.au/publications/pdf/png_appr_2007.pdf (accessed December 7, 2010); AusAID, "Australian Aid to Bougainville," July 2007, http://www.ausaid.gov.au/country/png/bougainville.cfm (accessed December 7, 2010); AusAID, "Aid Achievements in Papua New Guinea," July 2007, http://www.ausaid.gov.au/country/png/achievements.cfm (accessed December 7, 2010); Anthony Regan, "External versus Internal Incentives," *Accord* 19 (2008), 44–49; UNDP Papua New Guinea, "Fostering Democratic Governance," http://www.undp.org.pg/demogov.html (accessed December 7, 2010); UNDP Papua New Guinea, "Provincial Capacity Building Project," January 2007, http://www.undp.org.pg/Project%20Fact%20Sheets/dg/FS_PCaP_Project.pdf (accessed December 7, 2010); World Bank, "Worldwide Governance Indicators," http://info.worldbank.org/governance/wgi/sc_country.asp (accessed December 7, 2010); Asian Development Bank, Australian Agency for International Development, and World Bank, *Strategic Directions for Human Development in Papua New Guinea* (Washington, DC: International Bank for Reconstruction and Development and World Bank, 2007); Ministry of Foreign Affairs of Japan, "Structural Reform Program in Papua New Guinea," ministry

- **Local governance support.** Through the Governance and Implementation Fund (2004–07), the support for Provincial Financial Management Training Program (SPFMT) (1999–2006), the Provincial Capacity Building Project (2004–07), the Rapid Advisory Services Project (2004–07), the Bougainville Planning and Community Support Project (2004–07), and the Strengthening of Districts and Local-level Governments program (2007–12), targeted improvements were made in public expenditure management and development outcomes, public sector reform, and better coordination of donor assistance. These initiatives supported transfer of essential powers from the central to provincial governments. Training and institutional strengthening at the subnational level, especially for the Department of Finance, was emphasized. Mechanisms were established to allocate grants to lower levels of government and training and capacity-building were provided to local authority staff; supported by AusAID and NZAID, IDP Education Pty, UNDP, and the European Union.
- **Parliamentary support.** Support to the National Parliament project (2006–09) included activities to modernize and strengthen the capacity of a transparent Parliamentary Service, and enhance linkages between the national and provincial parliaments; supported by UNDP.
- **Audit and control.** Programs facilitated and built capacity of the Department of Treasury's Finance Inspections Division, Department of Provincial and Local Government Affairs, and Auditor-General's Office to achieve transparent and accountable polices; sponsored by the PNG Government, AusAID, the World Bank, and the Asian Development Bank from 2002 to 2003.
- **Public financial management.** Activities were conducted to decentralize budget monitoring and information to agencies, provinces, and local-level governments. Integrated trust accounting systems were developed, along with strengthened cash and debt management. Capacity-building training was implemented to manage and distribute aid efficiently; sponsored by the Asian Development Bank (ADB), AusAID, UNDP, and Government of PNG from 2007 to 2009.
- **Judicial reform.** Training was conducted of personnel in relevant state agencies to enable them to effectively and efficiently investigate and

---

report, 2008, http://www.mofa.go.jp/policy/economy/apec/conference/present0409/png.pdf (accessed December 7, 2010); Human Rights Watch, *Making Their Own Rules: Police Beatings, Rape, and Torture of Children in Papua New Guinea* (New York: Human Rights Watch, 2005); European Commission, *Forward in Partnership: Strategic Areas of Intervention for the European Union in Papua New Guinea* (Papua New Guinea: European Commission, 2007).

prosecute cases of bribery and corruption; between 2004 and 2005, programs were sponsored by AusAID, the Police, Ombudsman Commission, Auditor General's Office, Provincial Affairs, Finance and Treasury.

- **Electoral support.** Programs encouraged citizen participation in transparent elections and democratic processes through public awareness campaigns. They provided capacity building and technical support to the PNG Electoral Commission and improved electoral legislation, practice, and coordination across the PNG government on election budgeting and security; sponsored by UNDP and AusAID from 2005 to 2008.

- **Civil society initiatives.** Activities promoted a vibrant civil society that could contribute to sustainable community development activities. These programs advocated for shared development interests and concerns, and supported development of technical and management capacity for civil society organizations (CSOs). They supported capacity-building of faith-based organizations to promote accountable governance, peace-building and community participation in decision making and local governance; sponsored by AusAID from 2001 to 2008.

- **Media and public awareness programs.** These programs supported an open and democratic media to generate knowledge of and accountability from government. They strengthened the media, particularly radio capacities in rural areas. Public awareness of human rights increased through advocacy campaigns and human rights education. They strengthened existing human rights institutions, supported implementation of PNG-ratified international human rights accords, and supported the Ombudsman Commission. These programs educated the general public as well as leaders at all levels about the negative effects of corruption on society and the economy, and sought public support for legislative reform aimed at effectively preventing corruption; sponsored by UNDP, AusAID, Ombudsman Commission, and the Public Sector Anticorruption Committee in concert with civil society groups, business associations, and churches from 2002 to 2008.

Conclusions

Unequal distribution of resources and rampant corruption provoked the twelve-year-long conflict in Bougainville. Since the peace agreement in 2001, international organizations targeted their efforts at assisting in the peaceful and democratic development of the country and the Bougainville region in particular. However, due to a lack of sufficient funding, a mismatch of several aid programs, and severe destruction of state institutions, there has been a slow and uneven process of renewal and corruption control. This is demonstrated by the World Bank control of corruption indicator, which shows a 5.4 percent increase in corruption in Papua New Guniea as a whole between the time of agreement signing and five years later. Unfortunately, there are no independent measurements of change in corruption levels in Bougainville itself. Of the six country cases in this study, this is the only one that resulted in an increase in corruption several years after the peace agreement, despite implementation efforts.

One of the success stories in fighting corruption in Papua New Guinea was the establishment of the National Anticorruption Agency (NACA) and the training of investigators and prosecutors to engage the ombudsman commission and general auditor's office in their efforts. NACA is in charge of overseeing all major corruption investigations in public institutions and has arrested corrupt officials. This mechanism has promoted coordination of anticorruption activities among different anticorruption institutions. However, the agency lacks sufficient legal foundations to guarantee follow-up on anticorruption activities or to support the delivery of anticorruption legislation. Moreover, police and enforcement agencies lack the institutional capacity to efficiently undertake anticorruption measures.

Effective and efficient service delivery is also a major challenge at the provincial and district levels in Papua New Guinea. In this regard, AusAID and NZAID established the Governance and Implementation Fund (GIF) to intervene in the process of determining aid and national resource priorities and monitor the delivery of resources. GIF has contributed to prioritizing national and international investments in Bougainville's economic and political development and has supported finalization of the constitution and safe elections. More donor assistance is needed to properly support improved local governance practices in Bougainville after elections.

Additionally, UNDP has actively supported decentralization efforts in the country through utilizing and empowering local organizations to take ownership of local capacity-building workshops (for the Council of Elders), as well as providing on-the-job training for provincial treasury offices and creating a network of decentralization specialists. AusAID, UNDP, and the World Bank conducted technical assistance and capacity building activities in all major institutions to establish a transparent system of planning, budgeting, public financial management, procurement, payroll systems, and accountability. With their assistance, new management and audit systems have been established in all state departments in accordance with the Fiscal Responsibility Act of 2007. The financial management improvement programs have supported decentralization and effective budgeting and expenditure procedures on the national and subnational levels. The PNG government has established an auditor general under the constitution and restored the Parliamentary Publics Account Committee, two major institutions that keep government expenditure decisions accountable. However, these new systems have taken a long time to implement and remain rather fragile due to failed public administration reform, the absence of a strong and highly skilled workforce, and lack of strong department structures. The changeover in government staff also has diminished the effect of technical training and capacity building programs; the Support to National Parliament Project failed due to frequent parliamentary staff changes, miscommunication, and loss of institutional memory and political will.

To create political will and demand accountability, international aid organizations have invested in building constituencies for anticorruption reform and good governance. Civil society coalitions and radio programs have effectively reached people living in remote places. However, the exact effect of awareness raising programs remains to be seen. Consistent and long-term investment in the civil sector is expected to nurture continued demand for accountability and good governance.

8

Liberia

The war in Liberia began in 1989 with attacks orchestrated by then rebel leader Charles Taylor. This civil war was marked by brutality and atrocities and fueled by interethnic tensions. After a 1995 peace agreement, Taylor assumed the presidency in 1997 elections. His repressive policies and active support for the war in Sierra Leone catalyzed the establishment of another armed rebel movement, Liberians United for Reconciliation and Democracy (LURD), in 1999. Yet another armed opposition group, the Movement for Democracy in Liberia (MODEL), emerged in 2003.

The rebels' grievances included Taylor's continued interethnic brutality and suppression, repressive policies, and human rights abuses. Corruption was viewed to be at the root of the country's problems: Low salaries for civil servants resulted in endemic graft to receive public services, nepotism and favoritism were rampant, and public funds were stolen outright. The capture and exploitation of economic resources by warlord factions was clearly tolerated. By the time LURD was approaching Monrovia in 2003, there was significant domestic and international pressure for a cease-fire and a sustainable peace agreement. The Inter-Religious Council of Liberia and the Liberia Leadership Forum, both independent civil society organizations, called for peace negotiations with the Economic Community of West African States (ECOWAS) as mediator. By the time the agreement was signed, over 200,000 people had been killed.

The Negotiated Agreement

The Comprehensive Peace Agreement between the government of Liberia and the Liberians United for Reconciliation and Democracy (LURD) and the Movement for Democracy in Liberia (MODEL) and Political Parties, signed in Accra on August 18, 2003, was Liberia's fifteenth attempt to develop a viable peace agreement since 1989. Different from the rest in structure and content, the 2003 agreement covered a broad range of forward-looking issues in detail, including the establishment of a transitional government, institutional reforms, a human rights inquiry, disarmament and demobilization, and plans for national elections in two years. The agreement also included several basic principles related to governance in the postagreement period. It professed to be guided by principles of democratic practice, good governance, and respect for the rule of law as established in the ECOWAS Declaration on Political Principles of 1991 and the ECOWAS Protocol on Democracy and Good Governance, adopted in 2001. It also indicated an abiding interest in inclusive participation in governance, as well as promoting full respect for international humanitarian law and human rights.

The agreement starts off with an immediate cease-fire provision, including practical approaches for monitoring, disengagement, disarmament, demobilization, and reintegration. This is followed by a series of planned reforms and restructuring of government institutions, in part meant to enhance governance and reduce corruption. One of these reforms is the immediate restructuring of the national police force, the immigration force, special security service, customs security guards, and other security units. The reforms seek to establish greater professionalism in these services, emphasizing democratic values, respect for human rights, a nonpartisan approach, and avoidance of corrupt practices.

Another crucial governance-related element of the agreement is to establish a governance reform commission, specifically to promote good governance principles in Liberia. The commission's mandate was to review the existing program promoting good governance in Liberia, possibly to adjust its scope and strategy for implementation; develop public sector management reforms through assessment, capacity building, and performance monitoring; ensure transparency and accountability in governance in all government institutions and activities, including through the public ombudsman; ensure subsidiarity to local level governance through decentralization and community participation; appoint officials of quality and integrity while ensuring national and regional balance; create an environment that could attract private-sector direct investment; and assess the implementation and effect of activities undertaken to encourage good governance in Liberia, reporting findings to the national transitional legislative assembly.

A contract and monopolies commission was established to oversee the transitional government's work on public financial management issues. Its purpose was to ensure that all public financial and budgetary government commitments were transparent, nonmonopolistic, and in accordance with law and internationally accepted norms of commercial practice. Lastly, a reconstituted and independent national elections commission was included in the agreement to ensure that future elections were carried out freely and openly, guaranteeing the rights of all citizens.

The Negotiation Process

With the encouragement of civil society coalitions and the impending attack by the rebels on Monrovia, ECOWAS met with Taylor in early 2003 to begin discussing a new peace conference. Taylor chose the former president of Nigeria, Abdulsalami Abubakar, to mediate the June 2003 session, to be conducted in Accra, Ghana. The rebel factions entered the talks with a hard-and-fast position for the removal and departure of Taylor from office, though they assumed that he would not concede on this issue, but would seek a cease-fire and truce without leaving the presidency. Thus, even before the June talks began, it was easy to detect a future sticking point that could produce deadlock.

The surprise event, causing drama and controversy at the opening session in Accra on June 4, was the unsealing of the indictment of Charles Taylor for crimes against humanity issued by the Special Court for Sierra Leone. Although stakeholders' views of the event differed at the time, overall it positively affected the negotiations. The indictment delegitimized Taylor and immediately removed domestic and international support. He left Accra for Monrovia the next day, avoiding immediate arrest. The effect on the negotiations was manifest during the first two weeks of the talks when the cease-fire was concluded. It included a key clause removing Taylor from being a part of the transitional government and this enabled agreement by the rebels. LURD, MODEL, and the government negotiated directly to achieve this cease-fire agreement with no outside groups taking part.

Moreover, when the rebels heard of Taylor's indictment, they responded by shelling the capital. The fighting persisted during the Accra negotiations and served as a potent stimulus for achieving a cease-fire agreement. Some who participated in the talks indicated that the rebels used the shelling to extract concessions from the government at the negotiating table. That CNN was reporting live from Monrovia about newly launched attacks that were broadcast straight to the negotiators to remind them of the rebels' power gave rebel groups special leverage allowing them to push for useful trade-offs. This tactic was used to great effect during July and August 2003 after a draft agreement was distributed that sought to bar factional representatives from holding positions in the transitional government. The rebels' intense shelling assaults of Monrovia for three weeks resulted in an alternate mediator-brokered solution that incorporated the rebels into a large number of ministerial positions.

For these negotiations, the ECOWAS mediator, international representatives—primarily from the United States and European Union—and civil society groups were involved, in some cases pressuring parties to make crucial concessions. Some of the civil society representatives were official delegates, but many were unofficial observers; they did not coordinate extensively to promote common positions on key issues, which probably reduced their influence. Women's organizations—many representing the plight of refugees and victims of the fighting—were very active and often confronted factional leaders forcefully to stop the violence. They brought the realities and horrors of war to the negotiating table and insisted on speeding up the pace of the cease-fire talks. In addition, eighteen political parties were represented at the talks, the majority of which were aligned closely with Taylor.

The plenary discussions focused on arriving at broad principles on which all parties could agree. Once the formulas were achieved, details and the final text were developed offline and presented to the delegates shortly before signing, allowing minimal opportunity for additions or changes. No subcommittees were used to discuss the issues in depth, but there were many debates conducted informally on the sidelines of the negotiations.

International participants, who, with their broader experience, could introduce new ideas and options for consideration, drafted much of the proposed agreement text. LURD also actively made detailed suggestions for provisions. The ECOWAS mediator, to avoid controversy, would often remove sections from early drafts that referred to accountability. Provisions to reform the judiciary by appointing independent and temporary judges were seen as necessary and uncontroversial, and so were included in the agreement. However, proposals to strengthen the rule of law or review constitutional provisions were not included because international resources were not available to seriously pursue these areas in the short run. International participants suggested that these issues be discussed during the election campaign and in postagreement negotiations, after the transitional government's tenure.

Negotiation Analysis

Clearly, ongoing fighting in parallel with the negotiations was a potent way to extract concessions, rally civil society and international pressure on the negotiators, and motivate agreement on a cease-fire and beyond. The rebels used the war as blackmail to gain advantage at the negotiating table; cell phones and CNN coverage made this blackmail even more effective. If the fighting had been halted even temporarily as the peace negotiations began, the outcomes would likely have been significantly different.

The international mediator, along with the national civil society organizations, was important in keeping the talks on agenda and on track. Active rebel group participation in initiating drafts and proposals was a catalyst to introducing transparency and accountability provisions. International participants largely drafted the proposed agreements, as they had extensive experience in other negotiations and could introduce new ideas concerning governance, anticorruption, and other provisions that might have been outside the ken of most domestic participants. However, there was frequent turnover in the ranks of international representatives present at the talks and this hampered the pace of negotiation.

Despite the large role of international representatives, much of the content of the Liberian negotiations was homegrown. Local ownership of the ideas and provisions, plus the means to monitor compliance with the agreement, was viewed as leading to effective, sustainable solutions. Ultimately, the international participants decided to pull the plug on funding the peace talks once they saw that the bulk of the work was accomplished after more than two months of negotiations. A deadline was set and the remaining issues rapidly resolved or delayed for postagreement negotiation.

Implementation

Reform of the judiciary by appointing interim judges was an uncontroversial and little-discussed provision of the negotiated accord. The temporary judges were meant to replace the Taylor-appointed judges on the supreme court to keep the court free from political influence. The rebels pushed for other judicial initiatives among the negotiated provisions—including a legal reform commission to assess potential constitutional changes—but international participants quashed these ideas, fearing the cost required to follow through on this suggestion. By 2006, the law reform commission had resurfaced in serious discussions within the government.

During the two years of transitional government, donors were reluctant to invest in judicial reform until the government developed a detailed plan. However, some piecemeal programs were implemented, though they were not seen to yield the broader holistic changes needed. The legal and judicial system support division of the UN Mission in Liberia (UNMIL) trained prosecutors and public defense staff, and engaged a number of defense lawyers to represent indigent defendants. In 2005, the U.S. government provided short-term funding for a justice sector support program to train and advise public prosecutors, develop a public defense office, and assist with case management and financial oversight. The American Bar Association, also with U.S. government support, started a legal aid clinic in Monrovia. A governance reform commission and electoral reforms, agreed to at the peace negotiations, met with little resistance from the parties.

Other important programs were sponsored through donor assistance in Liberia in the postagreement period to implement various governance provisions of the peace treaty. A sample of these programs includes the following:[1]

- **Law enforcement.** The United Nations Mission in Liberia along with UNDP and UNPOL provided technical, capacity building, and logistical support to police forces through the Police Service Training

---

1. UNDP, "UNDP Liberia Programs," http://www.lr.undp.org/governances.htm (accessed December 7, 2010); UNDP, "2007 Annual Report: Democratic Governance: Fostering Broad and Meaningful Participation," http://www.undp.org/publications/annualreport2007/democratic_governance.shtml (accessed December 7, 2010); USAID West Africa Regional Program (WARP), "New Anticorruption Activities," http://www.usaid.gov/missions/westafrica/cprevention/newactivities/%20index.htm (accessed December 7, 2010); Neal P. Cohen, Charles Mohan, Kpedee Woiwor, James Whawhen, Sheku Daboh, David Snelbecker, *Final Evaluation of USAID GEMAP Activities* (Governance and Economic Management Assistance Program) (Washington, DC: USAID, 2010), http://www.gemap-liberia.org/doc/library/Evaluation%20of%20USAID%20Liberia%20GEMAP.pdf (accessed December 12, 2010); Martina Nicolls and Susan Kupperstein, "Final Evaluation: Building Recovery and Reform through Democratic Governance (BRDG)," USAID Liberia, 2006–07, http://pdf.usaid.gov/pdf_docs/PDACK649.pdf (accessed December 7, 2010); Creative Associates International, "Liberia Transition Initiative: Liberia Society Rebuilds," http://www.creativeworldwide.com/CAIIStaff/Dashboard_GIROAdminCAIIStaff/Dashboard_CAIIAdminDatabase/CAIIAdminProjectDetails.aspx?PageName=Liberia_Transition_Initiative&SurveyID=1042&ApplicationCode=1002&HighLight=LTI (accessed December 12, 2010); Human Rights Watch, "Liberia at a Crossroads: Human Rights Challenges for the New Government," briefing paper, September 30, 2005, http://hrw.org/backgrounder/africa/liberia0905/index.htm (accessed December 7, 2010); Office of the European Commission in Liberia, "Good Governance and Parliament in Liberia—Best Practices," Report by Konrad Adenauer Foundation, 2005, http://www.kas-benin.de/liberia/Rep_Basedau_Good_Gov_Dec05.pdf (accessed November 2010); John S. Morlu, "General Auditing Commission 2007 Annual Report," General Auditing Commission, Monrovia, Liberia, January 2007, http://www.gacliberia.com/gacannualreport_2007.pdf (accessed November 2010); United Nations Mission in Liberia, "Civil Affairs," http://unmil.org/1content.asp?ccat=civilaffairs&zdoc=1(accessed December 12, 2010); United Nations Mission in Liberia, "Legal and Judicial System Support" http://unmil.org/1content.asp?ccat=ljss&zdoc=1 (accessed December 12, 2010).

Academy and supported rehabilitation of Liberian National Police (LNP) stations; sponsored between 2004 and 2005.

- **Governance and awareness support.** Support was provided to the transitional government for education and youth programs. Grants were awarded to national organizations in the fields of justice, media, conflict management, good governance, and human rights, and technical assistance, and grants were provided to assist in effective planning, budgeting, communication and coordination. Support was also provided for regional activities to strengthen the Mano River Union. A code of conduct for public officials was formulated and support for decentralization efforts was offered; sponsored by UNDP, Swedish International Development Cooperation Agency (SIDA), and USAID between 2004 and 2007.
- **Audit and control.** Programs assisted the Supreme Audit Institution (SAI) to enhance and broaden the scope of training and information exchange activities through the establishment of a strong infrastructure. Staff were trained and coached on-the-job to ensure the sustainability and viability of audit training programs. Basic tools were established to undertake the fight against fraudulent practices and embezzlement. A regional capacity to assist SAIs in English-speaking Africa with forensic audits was developed; sponsored by the Ministry of Foreign Affairs (Netherlands), SIDA (Sweden), and the Southern Africa Development Community Organization of Supreme Audit Institutions from 2001 to 2007.
- **Public financial management.** The Governance and Economic Management Assistance Program (GEMAP) implemented a variety of economic governance projects to enhance transparency and accountability of state institutions. A principal anticorruption element of GEMAP involved appointment of international financial controllers in key state-owned enterprises and implementation of strict audit procedures and systems to ensure proper oversight and control of revenue collections and allocation of state resources. The controllers contributed to improvements in a host of financial procedures at state-owned enterprises, established clear rules, and produced manuals that incorporate these changes; sponsored by USAID, the World Bank, International Monetary Fund, and the European Union from 2006 to 2010.
- **Electoral support.** Programs were implemented to manage Liberia's Emergency Governance Fund (LEGF). These increased the capacity of the National Elections Commission (NEC) and supported civic

and voter education. Programs were created to improve economic and social conditions at the community level to reintegrate ex-combatants and mobilize communities for civil rights. Liberia's 2005 elections were assisted by support to the National Election Commission, political parties, and CSOs that encouraged political competition and free and fair elections; sponsored by UNDP and USAID from 2004 to 2006.

- **Civil society initiatives.** Assistance for West African Civil Society Networks supported improvements in communication activities and dissemination of anticorruption initiatives; sponsored by USAID and the Center for Transparency and Accountability in Liberia (CENTAL) from 2001 to 2007.

Conclusions

The fourteen-year-old interethnic war in Liberia was followed by moderate levels of international aid to support the transitional government after the peace agreement in 2003. Some of the initial donor funds focused on creating a civil society and mobilizing the youth, rather then investing in transitional government capacity building. However, due to pervasive corruption in government agencies, the World Bank, the United States, the European Union, and ECOWAS pressured the Liberian government to approve a three-year anticorruption plan—the Liberia Economic Governance and Action Plan (LEGAP)—to strengthen controls over economic activities by the government and key institutions. Over time, the Liberian government was also obliged to implement the GEMAP, which put financial control mechanisms in every major Liberian government institution and appointed expatriate specialists to author major financial agreements, control tax and revenue collection, and oversee the work of these agencies. The GEMAP mechanism is considered to have controlled financial transactions and fought corruption with measurable results. However, the budgeting process remains weak and closed to active citizen participation. Without an independent anticorruption agency or ombudsman office, corrupt officials can continue operations even under the GEMAP framework.

Increasing public awareness and mobilization against corruption is also seen as a success. The Building Recovery and Reform though Democratic Governance (BRDG) program has contributed to a massive information campaign to create public awareness of corruption issues and has resulted in more vocal demands for anticorruption activities from both international and local agencies. In addition, UNDP's support to the national election commission has contributed to safe and free elections in the country. The commission is autonomous and relatively free from political influence, but it still lacks sufficient staff to perform its duties fully.

Among donor-supported programs that have not been effective, the governance reform commission that was supposed to strengthen the accountability of governmental agencies and act as a public ombudsman does not have the powers typically assigned to effective anticorruption agencies that allow them to follow up on abusive practices. In addition, despite many donors' extensive efforts to restructure the police and justice system in Liberia and reestablish a predictable rule of law, legislative and judicial accountability is still considered to be weak.

Overall, though, the programs have had a cumulative and positive effect, according to the World Bank's control of corruption index. Liberia experienced a significant reduction (15.4 percent) in corruption over a four-year period since the agreement was signed. Of the six country cases, Liberia has experienced the largest measurable corruption reduction of them all.

Part II:
Analysis and Lessons

9

The Impact of Integrity Provisions

Does including integrity provisions in peace agreements improve the chances that postconflict countries will develop and stabilize their political systems and economies faster, while freeing themselves of the abuses and penalties of corruption? I quantitatively analyze the six preceding cases against a control group of seven recent postconflict countries where no anticorruption and good governance provisions were explicitly elaborated in their peace treaties. I selected the control group out of an initial list of twenty-one countries from the USIP Peace Agreements Digital Collection and the INCORE inventory of peace agreements according to several criteria: negotiated agreements ended their internal conflicts; the resulting peace took hold and was sustained; and there was no explicit mention of corruption, transparency, accountability, or integrity in the agreements' provisions.[1] The seven cases are the Nicaragua Agreement with Indigenous Peoples (January 26, 1988), Cambodia Agreement (October 23, 1991), Mozambique General Peace Agreement (October 4, 1992), and Tajikistan General Peace Agreement (June 27, 1997), as well as Angola's Lusaka Protocol (November 15, 1994), Croatia's Erdut Agreement (November 12, 1995), and Mexico's Chiapas Agreement (February 16, 1996).

No causal conclusions can be drawn from the following analysis and the very small sample size requires us to interpret our results with caution. Certainly, many factors at play in the aftermath of conflict can affect stability, growth, and political change.[2] But as the case studies emphasized, the nature of the negotiated provisions and their implementation in the postagreement

---

1. See www.usip.org and http://www.incore.ulst.ac.uk (accessed October 19, 2010).

2. See especially Jens Christopher Andvig, "Corruption and Armed Conflicts: Some Stirring Around in the Governance Soup," Norwegian Institute of International Affairs, Oslo, January 2008, on current methodological problems in analyzing causality between corruption and conflict quantitatively.

period are important drivers of peacebuilding dynamics. The analysis presented here tends to validate my hypotheses and assumptions that integrity provisions do make a difference. In general, comparison of aggregate indicators of official development assistance, corruption control, political stability, and economic growth reveals positive trends in outcomes for postconflict countries where reestablishing integrity was high on the agenda, more so than for the control group.

Data on official development assistance (aggregate aid in dollars) are gathered by the Organization for Economic Cooperation and Development (OECD). The economic growth data (GDP growth) are collected annually by UNDP. The control of corruption and political stability indexes have been collected by the World Bank Institute (WBI) since 1996.[3] The WBI indexes are derived by aggregating results from several citizen, expert, and enterprise surveys on key questions. The corruption index is generally interpreted as the extent to which anticorruption initiatives are effective in a country. Component questions include perceptions about public sector corruption and what is being done to reduce it. The political stability indicator is defined as the extent to which the quality of governance may be compromised by the likelihood of unexpected changes in government.[4] While there have been many critiques of these indicators, they tend to be considered among the best that currently exist.[5]

Attracting Foreign Development Assistance Funds

Do postconflict countries with explicit anticorruption and good governance provisions in their peace agreements attract greater donor attention and increased development assistance funding? Among all postconflict countries, the average annual rate of growth in official development assistance (ODA)

---

3. Daniel Kaufmann, Aart Kraay, and Massimo Mastruzzi, "Governance Matters VIII: Aggregate and Individual Governance Indicators, 1996–2008," Policy Research Working Paper no. 4978, World Bank, Washington, DC, June 29, 2009. The World Bank governance indicators database begins in 1996. Several of the agreements in our sample were negotiated a few years earlier. In these cases, data for the analysis were drawn from the closest year available. This problem is mitigated to a certain extent by the fact that the World Bank indicators are derived from component surveys that have been collected in years earlier than the date assigned to the index by the World Bank. Hence, data labeled as 1996 data by the World Bank might contain survey results from earlier years.

4. The World Bank Institute governance indicators can be used to assess longitudinal trends for individual countries, allowing those trends to be compared across countries; see Kaufmann, Kraay, and Mastruzzi, "Governance Matters VIII." Methodologically, global averages of these indicators ought not be compared over time, but country-level indicators have been constructed to facilitate cross-country comparisons and for evaluating trends over time.

5. Michael Johnston, "Assessing Vulnerabilities to Corruption: Indicators and Benchmarks of Government Performance," *Public Integrity* 12, no. 2 (Spring 2010), 125–42.

Figure 9.1. Average Annual Growth Rate of Official Development Assistance (ODA) (percent)

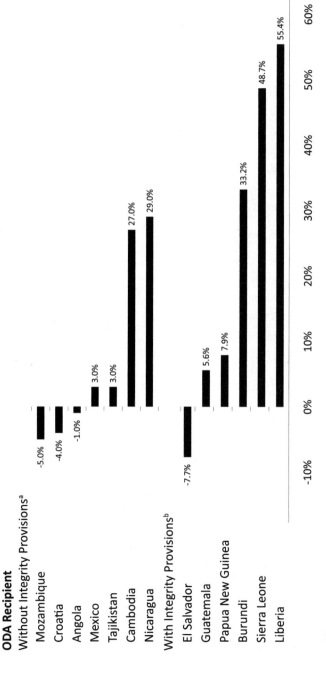

a. These countries saw an average 7.4 percent increase.
b. These countries saw an average 23.9 percent increase.

Note: The average annual rate of growth of official development assistance for each country is measured from approximately the time the peace agreement was signed to approximately five years later, based on data availability. A positive change indicates an increase in ODA levels.
Source: Organization for Economic Cooperation and Development, 2008.

varies greatly across five years after a peace agreement (see figure 9.1). But the findings demonstrate clearly that countries with integrity provisions fare much better in attracting foreign development assistance funds than do countries without integrity provisions. The former received an average increase of 24 percent, while the latter received an average increase of only 7 percent.

Among the six countries that included integrity provisions in their peace treaties, five saw modest to large increases in ODA, ranging from 5.6 to 55.4 percent. Guatemala and El Salvador, the earliest agreements in our sample (in the 1990s) experienced only a modest increase and a decrease, respectively, in the first few years after the agreement was signed. Bilateral and multilateral donors were much more generous with countries that negotiated their agreements more recently, especially Liberia, Sierra Leone, Burundi, and Papua New Guinea, which received very large increases in foreign assistance—for the three African states, much larger than the world average growth rate in ODA.

Among the seven nonintegrity provision countries, two in our sample received an average annual increase of 27 to 29 percent in ODA in the five years after their agreements. Of the remaining five countries, two experienced very small increases of 3 percent each, and three countries experienced decreases in foreign donor support, from −1 percent to −5 percent.

Reducing Corruption

According to the World Bank's control of corruption index, five of the six cases with integrity provisions—Liberia, Guatemala, El Salvador, Burundi, and Sierra Leone—have experienced a reduction in corruption over the five years since their peace agreements were negotiated. Only Papua New Guinea experienced an increase in corruption as measured by this index. Unfortunately there are no independent measures of corruption for Bougainville by itself. Hence, the countrywide index may not be adequately monitoring the actual corruption dynamics in the autonomous region in particular (see figure 9.2). Among the countries that concluded peace agreements with no negotiated provisions addressing corruption, only three of the seven countries experienced significant improvements in the corruption index in the five years after their agreements were signed, while four of the seven countries saw no changes or major declines (between 0 and −14 percent). The overall average for countries with integrity provisions increased by 5.4 percent, while the average for countries without integrity provisions declined by 1 percent. The

Figure 9.2. Change in Control of Corruption Index (percent)

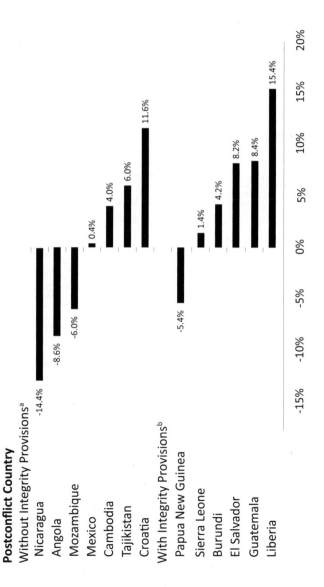

Postconflict Country

Without Integrity Provisions[a]

Country	Value
Nicaragua	-14.4%
Angola	-8.6%
Mozambique	-6.0%
Mexico	0.4%
Cambodia	4.0%
Tajikistan	6.0%
Croatia	11.6%

With Integrity Provisions[b]

Country	Value
Papua New Guinea	-5.4%
Sierra Leone	1.4%
Burundi	4.2%
El Salvador	8.2%
Guatemala	8.4%
Liberia	15.4%

-15%   -10%   -5%   0%   5%   10%   15%   20%

a. These countries saw an average decrease of 1 percent.
b. These countries saw an average increase of 5.4 percent.

Note: The percent change in the control of corruption index for each country is measured from approximately the time the peace agreement was signed to approximately five years later, based on data availability. A positive change indicates a reduction in corruption levels.
Source: World Bank Governance Indicators, 2008.

results suggest that including integrity provisions in negotiated agreements increases the likelihood of controlling corrupt behaviors and abuses in the postagreement period.

That said, all the scores, before and after the peace agreement, are well below the midpoint of the control of corruption index, so much more improvement is needed before corruption can be said to be under control. These countries are by no means anticorruption success stories. In Guatemala, for example, analysts suggest that the nature of corruption has been transformed from outright coercion to petty bribe-taking and fraud. But the integrity-provision countries appear to have benefited, at a minimum, by putting anticorruption issues high on the countries' public policy agendas, and in some cases by strengthening laws, regulations, and institutions to make corruption a higher cost–lower benefit behavior.

Improving Economic Growth

On average, the integrity-provision cases exceed the nonintegrity-provision cases in economic growth after agreement slightly, but the difference is very small, at 5.5 percent versus 5.1 percent, respectively. Both samples appear to demonstrate economic improvements as a peace dividend. Comparing the five-year period before the agreement with the five-year period after it, there are more substantial differences in economic growth for countries where there were no integrity provisions. This is not unexpected, as rapid rates of economic growth are quite feasible when countries are starting from a very slow or regressive rate.

All but one of the countries in the integrity-provision sample saw increases in economic growth in the years after their peace agreements compared with the years before (see figure 9.3). Guatemala, the only country that did not see meaningful economic growth after the peace agreement, at least remained relatively stable. These results also are not unexpected, since the preagreement period was characterized by violence and conflict that depressed economic activity. The rates of economic growth for four of the six countries in the sample exceeded or matched growth rates among Heavily Indebted Poor Countries (HIPC) for the same periods of time after the peace agreements. This is a substantial feat for countries just emerging from prolonged conflict. Only for Papua New Guinea and Burundi were economic growth rates substantially below the average rate for HIPC countries during the postagreement time frames.

Figure 9.3. Average Annual Growth Rate of GDP (percent)

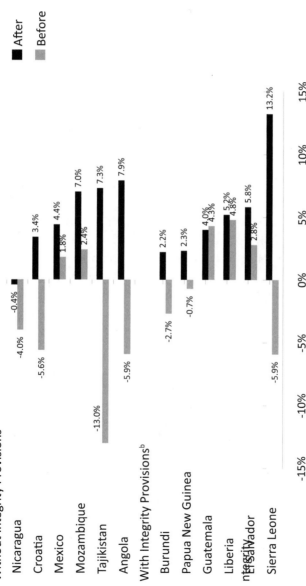

a. These countries saw an average increase of 5.1 percent.
b. These countries saw an average increase of 5.5 percent.
Note: The average annual growth rate of GDP for each country is measured from approximately the time the peace agreement was signed to five years before or after the signing. Data were not available on annual GDP rate of growth for Cambodia. *Source:* United Nations (http://data.un.org, accessed November 2008)

Achieving Political Stability

Have the two samples achieved differing levels of political stability over the medium term after their peace agreements? The World Bank governance indicator—political stability—measures perceptions that the government is safe from destabilization or overthrow by unconstitutional or violent means. Figure 9.4 presents the results for the countries with integrity provisions and those without such provisions. Except for Papua New Guinea, all countries in both samples saw improvements in political stability after the peace agreement. However, countries with integrity provisions showed a slightly stronger improvement, averaging a 16.2 percent increase in the indicator compared with an 11.5 percent increase among countries without such provisions.

Across all four indicators, the comparative quantitative analysis suggests that postconflict countries that included integrity provisions in their peace agreements generally fared better in the medium term. They receive a faster and larger ramp-up of foreign development assistance; apparently, donors see them as more attractive recipients of aid, with greater political will to implement reforms that result in more effective development and stabilization. Corruption reduction is also more likely among this set of countries. Again, the political will to make needed governance reforms is likely to be stronger, and the negotiated agreements have already elaborated a detailed vision of their path to accomplish such reforms. While economic growth patterns are relatively strong in both integrity- and nonintegrity-provision samples, the motivation toward and achievement of political stability is marginally stronger among the integrity sample of countries. Perhaps if the analysis were extended to observe changes over a ten-year period since agreement signing, economic growth and political stability might register more positive results for countries with integrity provisions.

Another consideration in interpreting these findings relates to the time periods when peace agreements were reached. Both the research literature and the policies of the major multilateral and bilateral donors seemed to embark on a new era of corruption consciousness in their lending and assistance programs starting in the mid-1990s. Four out of seven countries in the sample of nonintegrity cases occurred before 1995. In the integrity sample, five out of six cases occurred after 1995. This is a small number of cases, but the groupings suggest that corruption issues became more prominent for national and international actors in the mid-1990s, and this continues to the present day. Awareness of the importance of integrity provisions for future stability—and the necessary pressure to include them in peace agreements—has been growing in the diplomatic and development assistance communities.

Figure 9.4. Change in Political Stability Index (percent)

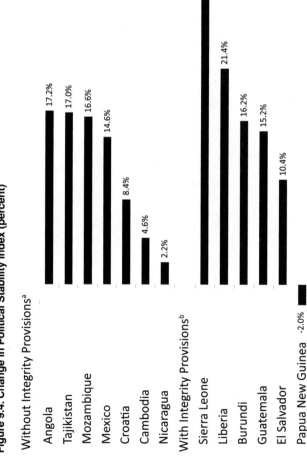

Without Integrity Provisions[a]

Country	Value
Angola	17.2%
Tajikistan	17.0%
Mozambique	16.6%
Mexico	14.6%
Croatia	8.4%
Cambodia	4.6%
Nicaragua	2.2%

With Integrity Provisions[b]

Country	Value
Sierra Leone	36.0%
Liberia	21.4%
Burundi	16.2%
Guatemala	15.2%
El Salvador	10.4%
Papua New Guinea	-2.0%

a. These countries saw an average increase of 11.5 percent.
b. These countries saw an average increase of 16.2 percent.

Note: The percent change in the political stability index for each country is measured from approximately the time the peace agreement was signed to approximately five years later, based on data availability. A positive change indicates an improvement in stability levels.
Source: World Bank Governance Indicators, 2008.

10

Lessons For Analysts

In the six countries analyzed above, peace was achieved through negotiations that included provisions to resolve some of the grievances that initiated the conflict in the first place: excessive corruption and abuse of power. The paths to agreement varied among these countries and some were more effective than others. Common features and trends—with either positive or negative consequences—emerge from comparing the cases.

Relating Negotiations to Outcomes

The agreement provisions and negotiation processes in the six cases produced a range of corruption and governance outcomes. Table 10.1 summarizes these findings. In all cases but one (Papua New Guinea), the control of corruption indicator showed an increase in the five years after the agreements were signed. This indicator roughly signals trends in corruption perceptions and appears to positively correlate with including anticorruption and good governance provisions in the peace agreement.

The largest improvement was seen in Liberia, which started from the lowest control of corruption score of any of the six countries; there, relatively detailed agreement provisions itemizing what needed to be accomplished after negotiations were matched by strong increases in early development aid, facilitating control of corruption. In Papua New Guinea, while the agreement was rather detailed, much energy had to be expended early after the agreement to physically rebuild the country and its institutions; this delayed a meaningful implementation of improved governance reforms.

Overall, however, there is no definitive relation between the control of corruption indicator and the degree of detail in the negotiated provisions,

Table 10.1. Summary of Six Negotiated Peace Agreements

Country	Negotiated anti-corruption provisions	Key features of negotiation process	Postagreement donor assistance	Evaluation of postagreement assistance process	Control of corruption indicator (World Bank, percent)*
Burundi	Detailed and explicit	Breakout into issue commitments; not totally inclusive	Major increase	Progress on paper, but not always in practice	+4.2
El Salvador	Explicit, but not extremely detailed	UN mediation; deadlines; shared interest in reducing military's role	Decrease	Slow progress; lack of strong political will to implement	+8.2
Guatemala	Basic principles, but not detailed	Formula led to details; UN mediation; reference to earlier models; external assistance carrot	Small increase	Partial implementation; weak mobilization	+8.4
Liberia	Basic principles with details on establishing commissions	Effect of ongoing rebel attacks during talks; influence of international drafters; details left to postagreement negotiations in commissions	Major increase	Slow progress; weak political will	+15.4
Papua New Guinea	Detailed on accountability mechanisms	Inclusiveness; trust-building due to length of negotiations; indigenous reconciliation processes; international interventions	Small increase	Slow progress, but persistent political will	−5.4
Sierra Leone	Basic principles with details on commission	Drew upon earlier very detailed, but failed agreement; strong regional mediation; promise of power sharing	Major increase	Very slow implementation and weak political will	+1.4

*Percent change in index from date of each agreement to five years later.

the nature of the negotiation process, the level of postagreement donor assistance, or the assessment of agreement implementation. There was much variation in these factors for each of the countries; it is in the way these factors combined in each circumstance that influenced changes in the level of corruption. The complex interaction of negotiation and implementation processes produced differing anticorruption outcomes over a period of years. The analysis that follows presents some common trends and lessons learned from the six cases about what does and does not work.

Negotiated Agreements

Some agreements include negotiated provisions that both explicitly refer to broad anticorruption values and principles *and* spell out detailed and specific reform measures, assignment of responsibility, and proposed timelines to implement those principles. Burundi's peace agreement is an example of this comprehensive and detailed approach. It covers anticorruption and good governance provisions, as well as reforms in a wide range of sectors and government functions: civil service, education, the judiciary, public finance management, and political party financing. The concept was to mainstream anticorruption initiatives throughout government. In addition, a commission to be established within the national assembly is responsible for overseeing the implementation of anticorruption reforms. Similarly, Liberia's peace agreement contains very detailed principles, plans, and reforms to address key governance and corruption grievances.

Guatemala is a variant on Burundi's theme. Its anticorruption and good governance provisions were the product of a two-year process, beginning with a broad framework agreement that presented basic foundational principles, set the agenda, and laid out the timeline for developing the rest of the agreement. This initial document laid out the root causes of the conflict and reform initiatives required across all sectors to develop the basis for peace and just governance. As in most framework agreements, ensuring respect for human rights was a basic overarching inspiration for all future action. Then, through a series of incremental agreements negotiated over the following years, a variety of issues were dealt with in detail, one by one. A UN facilitator helped to shepherd the agreement process, and each subsequent agreement detailed prescriptions and timetables for action in different governance sectors and functions.

Many of the peace agreements establish commissions with responsibilities to implement the anticorruption reform plan and monitor the initiatives' implementation and effectiveness. In some cases, it appears as if the commissions are an excuse for insufficient detail or likely lack of political will to outline the reform measures carefully in the agreement. This appeared to be the case in Sierra Leone, where a commission to implement the agreement and another to ensure accountability and transparency in the future use of natural resources were created in the agreement, leaving the details undefined and to be developed at some future time. Liberia, too, created several commissions in its peace agreement to carry out future reforms for transparency and accountability. These commissions could negotiate details and deal with areas of contention that could not be resolved in the preagreement period. They were vehicles for postagreement negotiation.

Establishing a cease-fire and a trusted way to monitor the end of hostilities is one of the first and common features of all modern peace agreements. Generating a physically safe environment is a reasonable prerequisite for good governance, anticorruption, and other peace provisions.

Several agreements were inspired by earlier agreements in their country or region. The Sierra Leone peace agreement was developed in the spirit of the earlier but failed Abidjan Accord, which was much more explicit and broadly sweeping in its provisions to deal with corruption and accountability issues. The ultimate agreement in Sierra Leone shied away from its more progressive predecessor, perhaps in fear of opposition to such an agreement, the likely inability to follow through with implementing such provisions, or the fear of repeating the failure of the previous accord. Guatemala's peace accord in 1996 was negotiated in the shadow of the 1992 El Salvador Chapultepec Agreement, and both were strongly influenced by the groundwork laid in the Esquipulas I and II peace accords of the mid-1980s. The anticorruption provisions in Liberia's agreement explicitly referred to the ECOWAS Protocol on Democracy and Good Governance. The Papua New Guinea agreement, while less broad than some of the other agreements in its anticorruption provisions, still drew upon international standards of good governance for the newly autonomous Bougainville region. Precedence here or there, failed or successful, is important in pushing forward new approaches to sustaining the peace.

Negotiation Process

The structure of the negotiation process must be arranged with care, as corruption needs to be addressed across a potentially wide range of settings. In Burundi, when talks resumed in 1998, Julius Nyerere reorganized them according to a detailed committee structure to deal with all major issues simultaneously and get all parties involved in the deliberations. Each committee analyzed corruption issues in detail within its own domain, mainstreaming anticorruption measures across several sectors. This structural approach, enabled by generous funding from Western donors, helped to disentangle issues of discord from one another and facilitated local ownership of the results. In El Salvador, the UN-mediated talks were also organized to treat each set of issues separately, although it was not a structured committee system, as in Burundi. In Guatemala, the range of issues to be discussed in negotiations were outlined in an overall formula at the outset, with a decision to deal first with the causes of the conflict and then with the operational issues of how to resolve them practically, through a cease-fire and institutional reforms.

In Papua New Guinea, the Bougainville People's Congress organized itself for upcoming negotiations in a more formal and systematic way, eventually yielding effective outcomes for their cause. It developed a position paper that analyzed all the options on all issues of concern in great detail, elaborating on a variety of possible futures and analyzing the interests of all factions. The findings were then discussed in meetings throughout the country to draw out further ideas and create consensus among all parties. In the end, the Bougainville negotiation position was very clear, powerful, and fully backed by factions that previously disagreed on the details of how to move forward. Eventually, it became the accepted agenda for negotiations with the government. The Sierra Leonean rebels were also very well organized and detailed in their vision for the future when they sat down at the negotiating table.

In Liberia, formulas were designed in plenary meetings, but the details and texts were developed outside of the formal negotiations, without much additional discussion among stakeholders. There were no formal issue-related subcommittees and international participants developed many of the texts. This resulted in a serious lack of detail in the provisions that ultimately became the agreement, and a lack of ownership by the government and local factions. All assumed that the details would be worked out later, during the postagreement transition period.

Finding a confluence of interests between governments and rebels is not always easy, but it is possible. In El Salvador, the new government largely represented the interests of economic elites who wanted to regain political power from the armed forces, while the rebels sought to end the human rights abuses suffered at the hands of the military. Both sides thus saw eye to eye. They jointly found a way to institute constitutional reforms that removed police functions from the military and put them in the hands of a civilian national police force. This redefinition of the armed forces immediately checked the military's unfettered powers in El Salvador and opened the door to other trade-offs.

Sticking points in the negotiating agenda can often result in deadlocks and a breakoff of talks, but in the best of situations, they can be resolved by strategic trade-offs. The El Salvador negotiations came upon an early problem: The government was demanding an early cease-fire before any other issues could be discussed, while the rebels rejected the cease-fire until their human rights issues were tackled. This was a clear recipe for stalemate. The barrier was broken when the government gave up its call for cease-fire in order to settle a structural agreement to subdivide issues and negotiate them separately. The government broke the logjam in Papua New Guinea also, conceding on a Bougainville referendum on autonomy in return for inclusion of good governance and anticorruption provisions in the postagreement period. In Guatemala, the initial threat that the army would become a spoiler subsided after a cease-fire was announced and the talks proceeded to substantive issues, thus reducing the army's involvement in the negotiations and increasing the involvement of business associations.

Meaningful deadlines can be useful to push talks to agreement. In El Salvador, the impending retirement of the UN secretary-general, who had been overseeing the negotiations, spurred the negotiators to reach outcomes earlier. External parties can also influence the proceedings, for good and ill. The promise of foreign development assistance is a positive incentive that can prompt negotiating parties to reach an agreement. The United States used this tactic in El Salvador, offering political and financial assistance for postwar reconstruction if the negotiations were concluded quickly. The early prospect of international financial assistance from the West also opened the door for negotiations in Sierra Leone to begin in earnest on difficult issues such as power sharing, cease-fires, and anticorruption reforms. Compromises were found on all these issues, but the limited participation of civil society, the failure of the cease-fire, and the failure of the international community to keep its word in providing aid led to the demise of the Abidjan Accords. In Guatemala, a final push at seeking a negotiated settlement was accompanied by significant international pressure. In addition to a UN mediator, external representatives from several supportive countries sat at the table. As a stick, a consultative group of donors threatened to withhold funding until the peace accord was actually signed. As a carrot, a UN mission was established even before the negotiations concluded as a confidence-building measure.

External incentives are not the only carrots that can advance the negotiation process. In Sierra Leone, the large economic rewards of the diamond trade were more than sufficient to cause several breakdowns of talks and keep the rebels fighting. In Guatemala, the heavy involvement of civil society organizations in the peace process—not as formal representatives, but as consultants on key issues for all sides—held out the promise of extensive popular support and was credited as a major influence on the final outcome.

Extended negotiations can serve many purposes. In Papua New Guinea, individual stakeholders developed relationships and mutual understanding over time that evolved into joint recognition for ordering the agenda; they could eventually agree that a cease-fire and physical security provisions had to come first. In Guatemala, the Esquipulas II talks that ended the Nicaragua conflict generated a national reconciliation commission for Guatemala to push-start a national dialogue on peace. This commission was built upon by the Lutheran World Federation to develop prenegotiation conciliation with the rebel group and opened the door for meaningful negotiation with the government. The negotiations in Guatemala lasted for such a long time that the informal contacts developed among the personalities at the table can be credited for turning the armed forces from a potential spoiler to a supportive stakeholder of the ultimate agreement.

When do peace negotiations become ripe for agreement on governance and anticorruption reforms? In Sierra Leone, the pullout of peacekeepers and massive rebel attacks on the capital signaled to the government that negotiation was the only available route. In Guatemala, after two years of hard-line talks that did not get very far due to tough, dug-in positions, it became apparent to the stakeholders that generally agreeable formulas existed, but it was a matter of splitting the difference on a range of issues. In Liberia, revelations of ripeness came from television cable-news reports of rebel attacks on Monrovia that were broadcast directly into the negotiating rooms.

Postagreement Implementation Process

Just as negotiation processes can lead in circuitous routes to agreements, implementation processes are often indirect paths to improved governance. The speed of the postagreement implementation process is a critical feature in reducing corruption outcomes. In Papua New Guinea, extensive and concentrated donor support, especially from Australia, boosted an early implementation process, though a lot of attention was focused at first on rebuilding destroyed infrastructure. But in Burundi, implementation was slowed, in large part because several outlier rebel groups still needed to be brought into the tent to sign cease-fire and power-sharing arrangements, removing them as potential spoilers of the peace. The final holdout, the armed wing of the FNL, finally disarmed and formally became a recognized political party only in April 2009, one year after signing a cease-fire agreement and almost nine years after most other rebel factions had laid down their arms. Rebel attacks in the meanwhile stymied implementation of many peace provisions. The postagreement transition period, which was originally negotiated to last for three years, had to be extended to five early in the process, and took even longer. Delays in implementing the provisions resulted in a waning of the enthusiasm and political will to deal with the corruption problem that was clearly evident at the time of agreement.

Delay also affected the fortunes of peace agreement implementation in several other cases. In Guatemala, many commitments were made in the negotiations concerning anticorruption and governance reforms, but these were not front-burner provisions. Operational issues to establish the cease-fire, demobilize combatants, and deal with refugees were first on the list. It took two-and-a-half years after the peace talks for the electorate to finally be presented with the constitutional reform package promised in the negotiated agreement. By then, passion for the proposed changes had diminished and the package was voted down, never to be reasserted.

Delay struck in Liberia as a result of international donor inaction. Waiting for the transitional government to produce more detailed plans, donors put their promised judicial reform programs on hold after the agreement. And in Sierra Leone, many reforms stagnated for four years after the peace agreement due to limited political will in the government. Active international assistance programs initiated governance planning studies, rebuilt infrastructure, and provided the resources to recruit and train officials, but government was reluctant to effect the reforms called for in the peace agreement, and civil society did not pressure government to pursue the initiatives.

Weak parties ultimately quashed hopes for effective implementation of the governance provisions in the Guatemalan agreement. The two parties that made commitments at the negotiating table both became progressively weaker after the agreement, losing hold of their constituencies. Within four years after the talks, neither held elective office and an opposition political party that had not been present at the negotiation table was voted into office. The new stakeholder group wanted to revisit the governance provisions from scratch.

The levels of international development and financial assistance have increased significantly in the more recent cases, offering the potential for adequately funded implementation efforts. Some level of donor funding and programming is typically provided after peace agreements are signed, but coordination among donors and with government institutions is not always effective. In addition, direct correspondence between these assistance programs and the agreement provisions can be faulty. As a result, there can be much activity with limited results in implementing anticorruption provisions. In Guatemala, much donor support flowed into reforming law enforcement, one of the key areas of the peace talks. However, local actors demonstrated limited willingness to reduce corruption. The government developed and adopted new laws, regulations, procedures, and institutions, but implementation in practice was lackluster. As well, in some situations—as in Guatemala—targeted international development support was well coordinated, but not matched by strong diplomatic pressure from the same donor governments to ensure that the assistance was backed up by imperatives to reform.

The above analytical findings can help in understanding how and why peace negotiations and their implementation were successful or not. They also suggest some lessons for practitioners that can serve to enhance future negotiations. These are outlined in the next chapter.

11

Lessons for Practitioners

Sustainable peace requires resolution of the underlying causes of conflict. Ending the violence alone through a cease-fire is not likely to suffice, nor is treating other symptoms of conflict likely to yield long-lasting results. A negotiation process must treat both the symptoms and causes together to provide postconflict societies with a truly new beginning. The cases offer some practical suggestions for both negotiators and the implementers of their agreements.

Implications for Negotiators

Negotiating provisions into a peace agreement that seek to control and reduce corrupt behaviors can stimulate targeted postconflict programs and international development assistance. Where this has occurred, our empirical findings suggest that corruption has been reduced several years after the agreement. None of these conclusions, by themselves, may appear to be unusual or unique, but together they constitute a set of propositions that negotiation practitioners should consider when negotiating peace agreements to promote the development and acceptance of anticorruption provisions.

Actors

- Including all key stakeholders early in the negotiations can produce progress in the talks and generate true and sincere buy-in to the agreement's eventual provisions.
- Excluding actors from negotiations can create spoilers when it comes to implementing the agreement.

- A respected international mediator can be a critical agent of momentum in a negotiation, raising the stakes for the local parties and making the talks irreversible. Mediators can also facilitate rebels' inclusion in talks, encouraging them to state their demands at the table. From their position in the negotiations, mediators can see the benefits of introducing anticorruption provisions and can find ways of promoting their inclusion.
- The international community and interested countries can be significant players through discrete interventions, mediation, and facilitation efforts. They can also provide a secure environment by deploying monitoring forces, while allowing for local control and ownership of the process.
- Civil society organizations can play several major roles in negotiations. They can be a forum to debate and develop detailed proposals on contentious issues that are then fed into the formal negotiation process after consensus has been found. Civil society groups can also provide the pressure needed to keep the talks on track to address an anticorruption agenda.
- Changing participation in peace negotiations over time can slow down the talks and threaten commitments to reach agreement.
- International participants with extensive experience in other negotiations can help in drafting agreement provisions, introducing ideas concerning governance and anticorruption that might be outside the ken of most domestic participants. However, if the representatives from interested countries change frequently and do not have sufficient backup and expertise in the needed specialties, their support can be suboptimal.
- Active rebel group participation in initiating drafts and proposals also can catalyze the introduction of transparency and accountability provisions. Local ownership of the ideas and provisions, plus the means to monitor compliance with the agreement, is most likely to produce effective and sustainable solutions.
- Rebel demands to end the current regime's corruption and abuse of power can easily be overtaken by their own greed and desire for power, thereby allowing the leveling of similar charges against the rebels in the future.

Issues

- A confluence of interest among competing factions in a peace negotiation, such as a common interest in limiting the authority and influence of the armed forces, creates opportunities to resolve many other issues, including those of governance and anticorruption.

- Structuring the negotiation process into committees and working groups, wherein each considers a different issue area in contention, can produce a systematic, comprehensive, and detailed agreement that incorporates extensive consideration of governance and anticorruption measures. By dividing the issues into manageable pieces, solutions can be found within each domain without the complexity of interacting with other contentious issues.
- Achieving a sustainable cease-fire is an essential prerequisite for following up with political provisions. If there is no agreement on a cease-fire, political measures can be delayed or not implemented at all. However, a cease-fire agreement can be made contingent upon all parties' acceptance that key political issues dealing with the root cause of the conflict will be addressed very early in the negotiation.
- The results of earlier failed talks can give life to new talks when the conflict becomes ripe for resolution, as the new talks can pick up on earlier innovations and progress.

Perceptions

- Public perceptions of government corruption are potent motives that initiate conflicts, but they can also serve to mobilize popular advocacy for incorporating anticorruption reforms into negotiated peace formulas.
- Developing a positive vision of the future for all conflicting parties can provide a sense of local ownership in it.
- It is productive if all sides to the conflict believe that they have won in the negotiation.
- Fears and suspicions of the other side can be adjusted as informal back-channel meetings produce greater familiarity and trust.

Process

- Trying to deal with anticorruption issues can galvanize divergent stakeholders into workable coalitions that can make the negotiation process more efficient at achieving results.
- Using a consensus rule in negotiation committees can become unworkable because of the large number of parties and interests that need to

be balanced, and the long time it takes to reach agreement as a result. International donors can easily lose patience with this process. Alternate approaches—coalition-building and softer consensus rules—can be introduced instead.

- Setting deadlines in the negotiations can spur progress and results.
- The extended time it takes to negotiate all the issues on an agenda can be seen in a positive light. Over time and many negotiating sessions, each side can learn a lot about the interests, difficulties, and reasoning of the other side, producing a sense of empathy and cooperation.

Power

- A government acknowledging power symmetry with the rebel parties can be essential in bringing the opposition to the table and allowing both sides to make the necessary concessions. With a perceived power balance, negotiation becomes not a process of victors imposing demands on the vanquished, but a channel to facilitate reaching a joint agreement.
- Power-sharing demands in peace negotiations can be used to introduce good governance and anticorruption reforms.
- If one or both sides to the agreement are very weak, endorsing a complex multidimensional peace accord may produce failure because neither side will be capable of implementing the negotiated provisions as intended. The best situation after agreement is to have a strong, but nonviolent, political opposition that can continue to demand implementation of the negotiated provisions.
- Rebels can make prominent demands to reduce corruption and improve governance, which are difficult for the government to reject without looking reactionary or irresponsible. The "shame factor" can play a useful role.
- Fighting that proceeds in parallel with the peace negotiations can be potent in extracting concessions, rallying civil society and international pressure on the negotiators, and motivating agreement on a cease-fire and beyond. Such fighting is usually to the advantage of the aggressor on the battlefield. Rebels can use ongoing conflict as blackmail to gain the upper hand at the negotiating table, and communications technology, such as cell phones and worldwide television coverage, can be used to further leverage an ongoing war. On the other hand, a temporary

halt to the fighting when peace negotiations begin can equalize power at the table.

- Indigenous reconciliation practices can be crucial to resolving conflict. Cultural norms of balanced reciprocity in traditional society can help to sow the seeds for compromises from all parties.
- Positive and negative incentives from external sources can spur the negotiation process, as international donor promises of future assistance can encourage governments to make the difficult but necessary concessions to arrive at agreements. As well, pressures imposed or predicted from neighboring countries and donor countries—such as the withholding of postconflict reconstruction funding—can motivate agreement on governance issues. Other incentives that external actors can introduce include early establishment of international support units that provide immediate postconflict support and verification of compliance with the agreement.
- If significant progress on formulating a peace agreement has been made, international participants can pull the plug on funding continued peace talks or set firm near-in deadlines, often stimulating rapid resolution of the remaining issues or pushing them off for future postagreement negotiation.

Formula

- An early framework agreement that establishes basic principles—a negotiation formula—can guide parties in discussing and agreeing on a wide range of issues, many of which often deal with the initiating causes as well as the effects of the conflict. Anticorruption and good governance principles can channel negotiation formulas toward forward-looking solutions and galvanize stakeholder support.
- Existing models of negotiation frameworks and peace agreements that worked in neighboring countries can motivate and inspire peace talks.

Implications for Implementers of Agreements

The implementation experiences of the six case studies, as well as recent research on postconflict reconstruction, yield some useful lessons learned for development practitioners involved in implementing peace agreements. Boucher, Durch, Midyette, Rose, and Terry's recent review of twenty-nine research sources revealed a basic consensus among analysts of anticorruption measures that are both appropriate and capable of success in postconflict rebuilding settings.[1] Table 11.1 summarizes their results, showing that post-conflict countries have tried a wide range of anticorruption programs, sometimes closely aligned with provisions in peace agreements. These include support for anticorruption institutions, legal drafting to repair deficiencies in the current legal framework, law enforcement, public financial management, audit and control systems, judicial reform, parliament, elections, local governance and public sector reforms, public education and the mass media, and civil society initiatives. While they offer interesting possibilities, the results of this study do not clearly differentiate programs for postconflict settings from typical development contexts. Moreover, they do not suggest any special program priorities for fighting corruption in postconflict settings.[2]

The six postconflict case studies presented earlier reveal the medium-term effects of implementing specific anticorruption measures in the postagreement period. Some had positive effects, others were only moderately effective, and still others appeared to fail. Table 11.2 presents the overall results.

Based on these findings, anticorruption programs that appear to be effective typically seek quick and positive results, transform training and institutional reforms into practical changes, and visibly enhance accountability and transparency. Programs that appear to be less effective tend to lack genuine stakeholder political will, experience factional squabbling, and fail to obtain the necessary buy-in from local political elites and other constituencies.

In the short term, the programs that appear to reduce corruption successfully seek to reassert or develop basic state legitimacy and effectiveness of government functions across all key sectors, in a comprehensive whole-of-government approach. This usually requires the strategic coordination of several donors with an allocation of responsibilities among them. They need to assure that

- basic public services are delivered;
- adequate legal frameworks are developed;
- the civil service is trained and professionalized;

---

1. Boucher, Durch, Midyette, Rose, and Terry, *Mapping and Fighting Corruption.*

2. Alternatively, USAID's Economic Growth Office has developed a very useful best practices guide that focuses on lessons learned in setting and promoting economic growth priorities in postconflict rebuilding countries (2007), most of which has the associated effect of increasing accountability and transparency in governance. Best practices are identified to support macroeconomic foundations, employment generation, private-sector development, agriculture, banking and finance, trade policy and institutions, and infrastructure.

Table 11.1. Research Results on Best Anticorruption Practices in Postconflict Situations

Goal	Anticorruption option
Criminal justice Legitimate, effective, and independent criminal justice system	Properly train and compensate judges, prosecutors, and corrections officers Establish professional legal organizations Establish whistleblower protection
Legislative and political Transparent and accountable political processes Significantly reduced incidence of cronyism and nepotism	Criminalize corrupt behavior Promote checks and balances systems (establish legislative oversight and ombudsman) Publicly report government activities and access records and meetings (establish freedom of information mechanisms) Establish codes of conduct, ethics, and disclosure rules as well as limits on immunity for public officials (establish inspector-general system)
Civil service Stronger and more capable public administration	Hold proper training, courses, and education of civil servants Pay salaries regularly Establish meritocratic and objective hiring, pay increase, and promotion criteria
Elections Political leaders with legitimate claim to authority	Establish independent election commission (monitor elections process) Create election rules pertaining to campaign finance and candidate eligibility (monitor political party compliance with laws)
Civil society and media Government held accountable to public opinion	Legally guarantee a free press Hold proper training, education of media, and standards of professional ethics Support civil society to hold politicians accountable (watchdogs) Educate voters Hold NGO workshops on politics and public responsibility
Public finance Sustainable and legitimate government revenue stream	Establish donor self-policing and aid conditionality (greater internal oversight of the use of public funds) Conduct regular audits Monitor procurement Keep monitoring agencies free from political manipulation Institute publish-what-you-pay regime Regulate and monitor currency and exchange rates Begin/resume tax collection, starting with customs (monitor tax collection and customs agencies) Manage natural resources property Secure borders with improved antismuggling measures (establish certificate of origin regime, end-user verification methods)

Table 11.1. Research Results on Best Anticorruption Practices in Postconflict Situations (continued)

Goal	Anticorruption option
Private-sector economy Effective government regulation and stimulation of the market economy	Lower trade barriers Improve/simplify permit and licensing mechanisms Make realistic forecasts Create job opportunities Provide market entry and exit mechanisms Encourage economic competition Encourage small to medium businesses by extending credit

Adapted from Alix Boucher, William Durch, Margaret Midyette, Sarah Rose, and Justin Terry, "Mapping and Fighting Corruption in War-Torn States," Report no. 61, Henry L. Stimson Center, Washington, DC, 2007, 26–27.

Table 11.2. Effectiveness of Anticorruption Initiatives in Six Postconflict Cases

Example of anticorruption programs implemented in postconflict settings	Typical outcome
Relative successes	
Audit and control: strengthened capacity through training and improved systems and infrastructure	Produces greater accountability, reveals ineffective expenditures, and expedites audits, but problems persist in audit follow-up
Financial management: capacity building through training and technical assistance in budget monitoring, cash and debt management, and Financial Management Information Systems (FMIS)	Yields more effective reporting and controls, increases in revenue collection, and greater budgetary controls
Civil society: training, grants, and assistance to provide public education, awareness of legal and human rights, and advocacy mobilization	Results in greater participation in policymaking and mobilization of advocacy campaigns
Media support: training to educate the public of their rights under law, investigate human rights and corruption abuses, and establish community radio networks	Media mobilized effectively to generate awareness of government abuses and citizen rights and advocate for speech and press freedoms, but legal threats usually persist against media
Moderate successes	
Local governance: capacity building in service delivery, citizen participation, and professionalism, and training in codes of conduct, streamlining, and improved administration	Builds cohesion and capacity, reduces ethnic and political barriers, and improves service delivery, but corrupt practices (especially patronage) usually persist

Example of anticorruption programs implemented in postconflict settings	Typical outcome
Judicial reforms: training for prosecutors, judges and court staff, restoration of the judicial system, and building court infrastructure	Cases adjudicated impartially, but slow process to develop qualified staff, improper influence by political and criminal sources, and high costs to bring cases to court. Judges often continue to be influenced by corruptive pressures and incentives.
Law enforcement: training and resources	Political influence on appointments and lack of citizen complaint mechanisms
Disappointing results	
Anticorruption institutions: anticorruption commissions, ombudsman, codes of ethics, filling legal gaps	Political interference in work of commission, little power to actually execute mandates, and insufficient budget
Electoral support: developing electoral commissions, citizen involvement, voter education, legal drafting	Political independence of commission questioned, electoral irregularities, and insufficient staffing. Generates raised expectations among the public that are difficult to satisfy
Parliamentary support: building capacity and professionalism	Typically, lack of political will and coordination to implement reforms

Based on development program assessments in postconflict Sierra Leone, El Salvador, Guatemala, Burundi, Liberia, and Papua New Guinea (see earlier case study chapters).

- accountability is established through checks and balances from both inside government (through auditing and controls) and outside government (through mobilization of civil society and media watchdogs);
- public finance systems are established and monitored; and
- regulations for business are simplified to facilitate the private economy.

Less effective initiatives are in the local governance, judicial, law enforcement, elections, and parliamentary arenas, where it is difficult in the short term to reassert independence from political influence and other traditional corruptive pressures and incentives. These also tend to be more dispersed functions and less conducive to evenhanded control across the board. Thus, implementers might find that they can succeed in some regions where there is political will as well as resources, while not in others. Attempting to establish new anticorruption institutions almost always fails to satisfy expectations because the institutions lack adequate mandates, authority, capacity, and resources to do the challenging job these agencies are assigned.

General Advice on Anticorruption Programming

While the above findings about particular initiatives can be useful, additional general guidance on setting priorities, deciding on who to work with, and sequencing reforms appropriately—all based on experience—can help the field officer make practical implementation decisions.

Strategic planning and sequencing of reforms. Overall, anticorruption measures ought to be incorporated into a strategic plan for stabilization and reconstruction operations, mainstreaming an anticorruption perspective into all initiatives. Experience shows that a multisector approach to fighting corruption tends to be more effective, as corruption is very resilient.

Immediately after a peace settlement, physical security, economic issues (e.g., jobs and basic policy reforms), and administrative issues (e.g., delivery of basic services) need to be addressed to establish a stable framework for recovery. These initial postagreement requirements mirror Maslow's hierarchy of personal needs—to satisfy physiological and safety concerns—but frames them at a state level.[3] In subsequent transitional phases, political and judicial issues ought to take prominence, along with reconstructing economic infrastructure and institutional capability. Not restoring these core state functions could lead to growing instability and the reassertion of corruptive influences.[4] Particular approaches to deploy early include the following:

- Strengthening and empowering primary state institutions and systems to operate under law; this can be accomplished without sacrificing accountability and transparency provisions soon after peace is achieved.
- Initiating early programs that will yield rapid and visible results, demonstrating that corruption is a high-risk, low-reward activity and that laws will be enforced. Initial strategies should support islands of integrity where they are found.
- Establishing a solid security and political framework early that raises the costs and risks of renewing violence.

Fighting corruption is a long-term objective but often requires short-term actions to address immediate problems and weaknesses in the post-conflict period. Short-term reconstruction timetables often increase reliance on existing power structures and newly created institutions, and may not allow for sufficient strengthening of fundamental governance reforms.

---

3. A.H. Maslow, "A Theory of Human Motivation," *Psychological Review* 50, no. 4 (1943): 370–396.

4. Harry Blair and Katarina Ammitzboell, *First Steps in Post-Conflict Statebuilding: A UNDP-USAID Study* (Washington, DC: USAID, 2007); USAID, *A Guide to Economic Growth in Post-Conflict Countries* (Washington, DC: Economic Growth Office, Bureau for Economic Growth, Agriculture and Trade, 2007).

Appropriate timing and sequencing of interventions is crucial and must be planned seriously.[5]

Urgency of response. Rapid and visible initiatives after peace agreements that seek to institutionalize integrity and significant anticorruption controls are desirable, and ripe moments for such anticorruption interventions come immediately after the agreement goes into force. At early stages, state institutions typically cannot implement such programs effectively, civil society is not organized enough to demand them, and international donors are predominantly focused on relief assistance. But the consequences of awakening late to needed anticorruption measures are an increase in the scope and severity of corruption problems, a spiraling public cynicism that the problem cannot be solved, and further destabilization.[6] A judicious plan to implement anticorruption measures should take into account the capabilities of the parties and what they can reasonably accomplish. Even small incremental steps in the right direction, if implemented effectively and visibly, can encourage skeptical partners and build momentum over time.

Donor coordination. Strong operational cooperation among donors and with host governments is essential so as not to overwhelm the rebuilding process and its fragile systems for delivery and accountability.[7]

Transparency. The principle of transparency is built into most successful postconflict anticorruption programs. Openness ought to be a major feature of these initiatives to engender greater trust and legitimacy. Public outreach programs about anticorruption initiatives can nurture public support.

Accountability. Independent monitoring and enforcement institutions must be established to demand accountability from and place limits on

---

5. Madalene O'Donnell, "Corruption: A Rule of Law Agenda?" in Agnes Hurwitz and Reyko Huang, ed., *Civil War and the Rule of Law*, Boulder, CO: Lynne Rienner, 2008; Jeanne Giraldo, "Post-Conflict Institution Building: Beating Corruption," Monterey, CA: Center for Stabilization and Reconstruction Studies, Naval Postgraduate School, 2006; Susan Rose-Ackerman, "Establishing the Rule of Law," in Robert I. Rotberg, ed., *When States Fail: Causes and Consequences* (Princeton, NJ: Princeton University Press, 2003); Derick Brinkerhoff and James Mayfield, "Democratic Governance in Iraq? Progress and Peril in Reforming State-Society Relations," *Public Administration and Development* 25, no. 1 (2005): 59–73; Mark Gallagher, "Building Fiscal Infrastructure in Post-Conflict Societies," Washington DC: USAID, November 2007; D. Rondinelli and J. Montgomery, "Regime Change and Nation Building: Can Donors Restore Governance in Post-Conflict States?" *Public Administration and Development* 25, no. 1 (2005): 15–23; Harald Mathisen, "Addressing Corruption in Fragile States: What Role for Donors?" Bergen, Norway: Chr. Michelsen Institute and U4; Frederik Galtung and Martin Tisné, "Integrity After War: Why Reconstruction Assistance Fails to Deliver to Expectations," London: TIRI, 2008.

6. Giraldo, "Post-Conflict Institution Building"; Galtung and Tisné, *Integrity after War*; Astri Suhrke and Torunn Wimpelmann, *Peace Processes and Statebuilding: Economic and Institutional Provisions of Peace Agreements* (Bergen, Norway: Chr. Michelsen Institute, 2007).

7. Rondinelli and Montgomery, "Regime Change and Nation Building."

political power. In a context of limited checks and balances, it is important to demonstrate early after the peace agreement that someone is monitoring the situation and that abuses of power will yield substantial penalties.[8]

Dealing with formal and informal governance. In promoting administrative reforms, donors need to deal with the reality that governance operates at multiple levels—some formal and some informal and corrupt. Amnesty for corrupt officials of former regimes can be considered, as this can halt continuing allegations of corruption and mark a departure from traditional ways.[9]

Decentralization. Measures to reestablish integrity in local governance may be compromised if local elites and administrative staff do not have sufficiently high levels of professionalism and resources. Promoting decentralization where the central government is weak, or there is extensive factionalization, should be considered cautiously. Concern also should be taken in restoring preconflict traditional authority in local governance, as this may not necessarily lead to good governance practices or legitimacy.[10]

Fiscal infrastructure. Reforming public finance procedures and institutions should be a priority for a rebuilding state because it is at the core of getting things done. Human resource constraints typically limit a government's ability to respond to demands for finance support and service delivery in postconflict countries. Reforms are typically needed in budget policy and programming, consistent with macroeconomic stability and resource limitations, designing public expenditure programs, operating the public financial management system, and creating a system of national accounts. Control mechanisms for public finances need to be developed to fight corruption. Statistical information systems should be a prerequisite for any fiscal reform program. Urgent reforms should include expenditure controls, receipts management, indirect tax controls, and the capacity to handle fiscal policy.[11]

Postconflict countries generally have weak tax collection systems and, as a result, government revenues are typically low. International or shared administration of customs and other economic agencies that are being re-

---

8. Rose-Ackerman, "Establishing the Rule of Law."

9. Lister and Wilder, "Strengthening Subnational Administration"; U4 Anti-Corruption Resource Center, "Sequencing of Anti-corruption Measures in Post-Conflict Countries," www.u4.no (accessed October 19, 2010).

10. Paul Jackson, "Chiefs, Money, and Politicians: Rebuilding Local Government in Post-War Sierra Leone," *Public Administration and Development* 25, no. 1 (2005): 49–58; Brinkerhoff and Mayfield, "Democratic Governance in Iraq?"

11. Gallagher, "Building Fiscal Infrastructure"; U4, "Sequencing of Anti-Corruption Measures."

formed may produce increased revenue collection, but may not affect anticorruption goals.[12]

Public awareness. Public education programs on the costs of corruption and anticorruption measures should be promoted hand in hand with capacity building reform programs. Awareness will help to mobilize popular trust in government if effective countermeasures actually reduce corruption. Otherwise, awareness by itself can increase citizen frustration and cynicism, as well as public perceptions that corruption is on the rise as reconstruction programs progress.[13]

What to avoid. Feedback from practitioners on what to avoid includes the following:

- Donors should not place large demands on reformers that overwhelm their capabilities and those of the fragile state. An incremental approach to reforms is more in tune with the limited capacity of postconflict situations.
- Dedicated anticorruption agencies typically are ineffectual unless they are given full prosecutorial powers and sufficient funding for at least ten years. There must also be functioning asset declaration procedures for all senior officials and an enforcement strategy that is a component of broad institutional reforms.
- Premature concentration on democracy and elections can lead to destabilization and renewal of the conflict.
- Economic conditions are unlikely to improve unless the legal building blocks for open economic activity are in place.
- Early privatization of state assets can unintentionally create an entrenched class of corrupt officials.

Planning and Operational Considerations

The postconflict rebuilding situation presents many sensitivities and potential pitfalls that need to be considered carefully in programming for effective anticorruption initiatives. For example, the World Bank grounds its operational strategies for Low-Income Countries Under Stress (LICUS) on seven principles:[14]

---

12. O'Donnell, "Corruption: A Rule of Law Agenda?"; Gallagher, "Building Fiscal Infrastructure."

13. Rose-Ackerman, "Establishing the Rule of Law"; Gallagher, "Building Fiscal Infrastructure"; Galtung and Tisné, *Integrity After War.*

14. Carvalho, *Engaging with Fragile States.*

- staying engaged despite downturns and disappointments
- anchoring strategies in a strong sociopolitical assessment
- promoting domestic demand and capacity for change
- supporting simple and feasible entry-level reforms
- exploring innovative mechanisms for social service delivery
- working closely with other donors
- measuring and monitoring results

Applying these principles, the World Bank's business model for addressing postconflict countries emphasizes, first, the rapid and visible rebuilding of effectiveness and state capacity, including administrative training and institution building to support revitalization of service delivery and economic development, and second, the legitimacy and accountability of the state, including oversight mechanisms in government and from civil society.

Assessing the Problem. It is important to understand both a country's particular vulnerabilities to corruption after conflict and its readiness to engage in anticorruption programs. Before programming, a thorough assessment of vulnerabilities and readiness should be conducted to determine priority areas that need to be addressed and opportunities and obstacles that might affect program implementation. The assessment should incorporate a political and economic analysis of the situation to tap the underlying causes of corruption problems, not just its symptoms. If possible, conducting joint assessments in coordination with other involved donors could get multiparty buy-in to the conclusions, including the parties to the peace agreement.[15]

The numerous risks in postconflict settings and the limited capacity of most rebuilding countries to counter these risks present a clear tension for the development professional. Priorities must be set, and assessments of corruption risks can help to determine if weaknesses are sufficiently serious to warrant special anticorruption programming. Table 11.3 presents a sample set of questions for such an assessment. A significant number of affirmative answers to the questions would suggest that programmatic action should be taken. If legitimacy is lacking, anticorruption initiatives are probably required to build citizen confidence and trust in government. If effectiveness is lacking, anticorruption programs need to focus on strengthening the legal, administrative, and institutional frameworks of government.

Assessing a postconflict country's readiness for meaningful anticorruption activity must account for the difficulties that the situation after conflict presents, while evaluating the facilitating or inhibiting roles of external actors as

---

15. Mathisen, "Addressing Corruption in Fragile States."

Table 11.3. Key Corruption Risk Assessment Questions

Legitimacy: assessing citizen confidence and trust in government
1. Are spoiler factions present and mobilized?
2. Are there inadequate accountability and controls for government expenditures?
3. Is top leadership perceived to be corrupt?
4. Is there limited political will to implement tough anticorruption measures?
5. Are civil society and the mass media weak and unprepared to advocate actively to pressure government for reforms?

Effectivenes: assessing the strength of legal, administrative, and institutional government work
1. Is there an atmosphere of violence, lawlessness, and impunity in society?
2. Are political and economic elite poised to take advantage of the current transition and grab state resources?
3. Is the state suffering from diminished capacity to govern and provide basic services to the public?
4. Is the state unable to absorb the massive influx of development assistance being provided by foreign donors in a transparent and accountable fashion?
5. Is petty corruption visible, acknowledged, and widespread?
6. Is the economic sector plagued by the absence of effective and enforceable laws and regulations?
7. Is corruption entrenched in the high-risk sectors mentioned above?

well. The questions in table 11.4 can serve as the basis for an assessment of a country's readiness for significant anticorruption programs.

Evaluating a country's readiness status to deal with corruption can help development practitioners design effective strategies. Figure 11.1 presents examples of relevant strategies in the face of high versus low readiness, and legitimacy versus effectiveness risks. Obviously, low readiness inhibits what can be accomplished, but this need not halt anticorruption programming. Basic capacity-building activities can yield fruit over time and when political will shifts. That said, high readiness bodes well for more aggressive and substantial anticorruption initiatives.

Mainstreamed initiatives. Anticorruption efforts should be embedded into all stabilization and reconstruction initiatives. Primary anticorruption activities should be targeted at security, economic, and administrative programs, with an underlying foundation of a mutually accepted legal framework. Political and judicial initiatives are typically meaningful at a secondary stage.

Multisectoral approach. Overall, a comprehensive multisectoral anticorruption program is appropriate in most cases; it seeks to ensure that corruption does not merely migrate to another less protected venue. Such whole-of-government program approaches should seek to encourage accountability and transparency. Efforts that target reforms at the local level are often

Table 11.4. Key Readiness Assessment Questions

Opportunities for readiness	Obstacles to readiness
Did the peace agreement include explicit anti-corruption or good governance provisions?	Are there serious questions about the government's legitimacy? Are there questions about the government's authority to govern, limited accountability, limited rule of law, and minimal inclusiveness of citizens in decision making?
Are there obvious champions for anti-corruption reform in or out of government?	Is security still a problem? Is there frequent lawlessness, violence, and impunity, and is the state a kleptocracy with excessive greed exhibited by the ruling elites?
Are there external pressures on the government to initiate and implement anticorruption reforms? Are external actors providing sufficient and targeted funds and assistance?	Are there serious questions about the effectiveness of the state? Does the state suffer from a limited capacity to perform, deliver and govern? Is petty corruption widespread? Is the informal economy thriving?
Is there forceful internal demand for change and reform?	Are external actors contributing to the problem?
Is there a meaningful existing framework for anticorruption reforms (that is, laws, regulations, institutions, procedures)?	

successful because they motivate stakeholders to act where they experience corruption the most and in a direct and personal way.

Balanced programs. Programs should balance supply- and demand-side reforms—that is, activities that address government deficiencies on one hand and boost citizen, media, and business efforts on the other. If legitimacy is the problem and readiness is low, demand-side programs are more relevant; citizens need to mobilize and keep anticorruption issues high on the public agenda. When state effectiveness is the problem and readiness is high, supply-side programs are most relevant that strengthen institutional capacity to deliver services and enhance legal frameworks to prevent abuses.

Timing. Rapid rollout of anticorruption programs is critical. It takes advantage of the euphoria after a peace agreement and also engages the stakeholders whose political will for such reforms is still strong. Waiting to implement anticorruption programs often results in failure. Appropriate sequencing of initiatives is also critical in postconflict countries because of the fragility of institutions and the fear of resurgent violence.

Figure 11.1. Assessing Corruption Risks and Anticorruption Readiness to Develop Targeted Strategies

READINESS

		Low readiness	High readiness
RISKS	**Legitimacy problems**	Strengthen civil society organizations Initiate public awareness/ education programs	Train and organize citizen watchdogs Promote investigative journalism
	Effectiveness problems	Reestablish basic public service delivery Fill in gaps in legal/regulatory framework	Strengthen judicial sector and parliamentary oversight Build public finance and local governance systems

Coordination. Many donors, governments, international and regional organizations, and private voluntary organizations converge on postconflict countries to provide assistance and resources at a time when these countries have the least capacity to absorb large amounts of support. To avoid doing further harm to these fragile states, it is crucial to coordinate efforts with other providers to ensure that the rapid and massive influx of international assistance does not result in theft or abuse.

Also, in the rush to support postconflict countries, it is important to allocate responsibilities for the various sectoral and functional reform initiatives to prevent duplication of efforts. The content of messages sent to the host country from external actors must be controlled; mixed messages about corruption from different actors can allow the host government to play one off against the other. Finally, donor assistance works best if it is locally driven and if there is popular demand for change.

Measuring effects. Realistically, anticorruption programs are not likely to generate rapid success stories and highly significant quantifiable outcomes in the short term. Instilling a culture of integrity, especially in a fragile rebuilding setting, takes time and patience. However, small but important short-term results, if detected, can motivate donors, host governments, and local implementers alike. Project-level indicators that show incremental improvements should be sought in the short run, with a long-term view of five to ten years for more substantial anticorruption outcomes. Publicizing such results can go a long way to enhancing citizen confidence in government and reducing perceptions of widespread corruption.

12

Achieving Peace with Integrity

Peace negotiations are principally a means to end violent conflicts, but they can achieve much more. Once there is consensus to stop the fighting, peace negotiations can begin to focus on the country's future: reconstruction, strengthening of economic and governing institutions and processes, stabilization, and normalization. Negotiations can be oriented toward such forward-looking goals if stakeholders are motivated to overcome grievances that were at the core of the initial conflict. Often with outside mediation, a comprehensive formula can be cobbled together that presents a vision to right past wrongs and, in doing so, reconstitutes an economic and governance system that is open, accountable, and invites participation by all. Such a formula outlines a future incorporating justice and peace.

Controlling corruption and abuse is central to such a vision of a country's future. These adversities—often among the grievances that instigated conflict—thrive in the uncertainty and change of postconflict societies. Without proper control, corruption can cause a peacebuilding situation to backslide into conflict and instability. Negotiated peace formulas need to consider vulnerabilities to corruption and abuse in their societies and develop detailed ways to prevent, control, and minimize such risks. As the cases in previous chapters demonstrate, negotiating a good forward-looking agreement cannot by itself guarantee peace with controlled corruption; how the agreement is implemented is just as crucial as arriving at successful outcomes. A principal factor in this regard is the amount, speed, nature, sequencing and coordination of international development assistance. Foreign donors, as well as the host government and civil society, must focus their programs on implementing provisions that have been negotiated quickly while political and good will are fresh. All parties must also make long-term commitments to implement the provisions. Achievements in the short term are likely to be invigorating, but may represent only small steps in the right direction. Giving up too soon is all too common in the international development field; there are always new targets for foreign assistance and domestic pressures to show dramatic effect. But withdrawing resources prematurely may doom the peace process to an indeterminate conclusion.

Rarely is implementation an orderly process. Learning about what works and what does not, where the peace agreement left gaps and where new solutions are still needed, is typical. Thus, postagreement negotiations are essential to extend, revise, and refine the original peace treaty during implementation in response to the postconflict country's fluid political and economic situation. Such talks also bring the former combatants together in a continuing forum to solve the country's problems and learn more about the other side's interests and needs. Most important, they reconstitute a critical element of any well-functioning democratic government: the participation of interested parties in developing decisions and future policy through peaceful dialogue and compromise.

Moving from confrontation to a culture of negotiation is the essence of President John F. Kennedy's image of a sustainable government. To him, negotiation is the essence of democratic decision making.[1] Making public policy requires compromise among the demands and desires of all stakeholders. It cannot tolerate rigid or inflexible positions; responsible legislators and government managers in a democratic system must be flexible, willing to adjust and modify positions to find mutual accommodation among stakeholders in a pluralistic society. This is not to say that government decision makers or advocates from other factions must abandon their principles, values, and beliefs. It is just that the art of getting things done in a democracy requires balancing multiple perspectives and interests, rather than having one interest overpower all alternative positions, and this can be done through the mutual concessions made in the give and take of negotiations.

Starting the Process

What, according to the cases, motivates stakeholders in internal conflicts to initiate discussions of integrity provisions during the negotiation process and include them in peace agreements?

---

1. John F. Kennedy, *Profiles in Courage* (New York: Harper Perennial, 1956), 5–7.

First, stakeholders often turn to negotiation when they have reached a hurting stalemate after prolonged and brutal conflicts.[2] In the cases discussed earlier, the parties perceived that the conflict had become ripe for resolution—when, as in Zartman's terms, they sensed that they have reached a mutually hurting stalemate (in terms of the fighting) or an overwhelmingly rewarding opportunity (in terms of promised foreign assistance) that made it illogical to continue the conflict. At this realization, all sides appeared to be willing to negotiate not only a cease-fire, but a more forward-looking solution. They were ready to look back at what caused the conflict and look forward to what they could do to fix those problems. Both former combatants and external participants in the peace process recognized that the underlying causes of conflict were still prominent and in need of resolution, emphasizing political over military, or imposed, solutions to the conflict. In other words, they were ready to negotiate to formulate a comprehensive solution incorporating good governance, and hopefully, stability.

It is not enough for the parties to only understand that the time is ripe for resolving their deeply held differences; they need to have creative ideas to reasonably address those problems.[3] While local factions can generate such ideas, a major source of innovation also can come from interested external parties, such as neighboring states, international and regional organizations, major powers, and non-governmental groups. When they serve as formal or informal mediators, experts, or observers at the negotiations, they can intercede with their expertise, experiences, lessons learned, and best practices from peace processes in other countries and historical conflict resolution efforts. Local combatants are more likely to view ideas transferred into the conflict zone by neutral external parties as novel, acceptable, and worth a try. That said, in the long term, there must be local ownership of such ideas to ensure their sustainability.

External mediators and donors also catalyze the inclusion of integrity provisions by offering critical carrots and sticks during the negotiation process. They can imply—or threaten—that future donor assistance will be withheld if good governance provisions are not integral elements of the peace agreement. Alternately, they can promise assistance programs, resources, investment, and trade if such provisions are included. As well, they can help to

2. I. William Zartman, "The Timing of Peace Initiatives: Hurting Stalemates and Ripe Moments," in John Darby and Roger McGinty, eds., *Contemporary Peacemaking: Conflict, Violence and Peace Processes* (Basingstoke, UK: Palgrave Macmillan, 2003), 19–29.

3. Bertram Spector, "Creativity Heuristics for Impasse Resolution: Reframing Intractable Negotiations," *The Annals of the American Academy of Political and Social Science* 542, no. 1 (November 1995): 81–99.

realize integrity provisions by making sure that their financial and technical support is recognized in the peace agreement to support future implementation of the provisions.

Active civil societies can apply significant pressure at or near the negotiation table to keep anticorruption issues high on the peace agenda. With strong political will to improve future governance and eliminate corruption, civil society groups are motivated to demand such provisions in the peace agreement.

The very structure of the peace negotiation process can promote inclusion of integrity provisions. When the talks are parceled out to issue-based committees, cogent solutions can often be designed for even the most sensitive problems. Certainly, if corruption were among the initiating grievances of the conflict, it would have a prominent position among the issues being discussed. The more inclusive the negotiations are in terms of bringing all the conflicting parties to the table, the more likely that integrity provisions will be raised.

Lastly, a powerful motive to include integrity provisions is the shame factor. How can parties to the negotiation publicly condone corruption or reject including integrity provisions that are so clearly beneficial to the larger public? If governments resist including anticorruption provisions in the peace agreement, they may be viewed as endorsing past and future corrupt behavior. If at least one party to the negotiation introduces cogent anticorruption provisions, it may be too difficult or embarrassing for any other party to oppose their inclusion in the final treaty.

Negotiation Process

Once started, the peace negotiation process ought to operate according to several key principles: inclusion, external participation, comprehensiveness, and attention to detail.

Inclusion. Every attempt should be made to ensure that all factions are included in the peace talks and have an opportunity to state their positions and make their demands. Hopefully, through the negotiation process, they can buy in to the outcome and be committed to implementing it. Excluding one or more factions can create an opening for spoilers of the peace.

External participation. Outside parties can contribute in many ways to the peace negotiations. As mentioned above, they can motivate innovation by injecting new ideas into the process. They can speed up the process by introducing deadlines. They can also influence the issues considered and the shape of the final outcome by wielding their sticks and carrots.

Comprehensiveness. Attention to the initiating and underlying causes of the conflict, including corruption and abuse of power, necessitates a comprehensive, multifaceted, and whole-of-government negotiation formula. If corruption is reduced in one sector or at certain government levels, it often reappears in other sectors or levels. International experience has shown that corruption is resilient, and countries must develop comprehensive programs to fight it. To date, peace agreements that have had the foresight to include anticorruption provisions have not been comprehensive in scope; they most often target corruption in the judicial sector or recommend establishing an anticorruption commission, for example, because these reforms are seen as attacking the most vulnerable aspects of the system. But even if the agreed-upon reforms are implemented as intended, it does not necessarily portend major reductions of corruption in the country. As some of the measurements indicate, even the most sincere efforts made by the government, citizens, and the international community can do very little in reducing widespread corruption. In fact, corruption may increase and reappear in another sector.

Attention to detail. Experience has shown that vague or imprecise provisions are not very useful. The more specific and detailed the formulations, the more implementable they are. Broad statements of principles about good governance and fighting corruption, that are not followed up by more detailed actions in the agreement, and responsibilities for their implementation may only delay accomplishment while the parties debate them later on. It is worth spending the time during the peace talks to introduce and agree on detailed approaches to achieve the broader principles of integrity.

Prerequisites. The institutions of the state and economy must be strengthened; they are essential prerequisites for success in implementing integrity provisions. Fragile institutions and weak procedures for their operation only encourage abuse and misconduct. If integrity provisions are to be implemented and the peace process is to yield a stable future, well-structured institutions need to be backed up by a trained and professional civil service, public administration standards, and audit and control mechanisms that keep government decisions and actions transparent and accountable to the public. Since many of these government and economic institutions typically provide public services, they are among the first that can evoke an image of competence, trust, and legitimacy for the newly invigorated government. Such public perceptions are crucial to government acceptance and stability in the early, fragile days after a peace agreement is signed.

Development Assistance Programs

Several major principles should guide development assistance responses after the peace agreement is signed: rapid response, sequencing, coordination, and local ownership.

Rapid response. Experience shows that there is a limited amount of time after the peace treaty is signed within which the goodwill of the agreement and the negotiation process supports and motivates effective implementation of the provisions. Donors need to properly align their resources and capabilities to facilitate quick action once the agreement is signed.

Sequencing. Establishing physical security is clearly the first order of business after the peace agreement is signed. But soon after that, the host government and donors should immediately begin the second phase of reconstruction and stabilization—rebuilding administrative institutions and delivering public services with integrity. Once this is begun, and overlapping with it, the next phase of assistance can commence: reforms to the economic, political, and judicial sectors that include transparency and accountability provisions. Donors often indicate that, after agreement, they cannot or will not disburse the promised financial support to implement the agreement until general security and stability is achieved. While this is certainly understandable if the cease-fire is not holding and violence persists, long postponements and delays in funding institutional development reform programs, such as anticorruption initiatives, can themselves contribute to further destabilization by not correcting what are often the core problems that caused the internal conflict to start with.

Coordination. Many donors are often mobilized to support the rebuilding of postconflict countries, which can lead to a problem of coordination among donors themselves, as well as between donors and host governments. The rapid ramp-up of funding and vast resources made available during the early implementation period makes this rebuilding stage extremely vulnerable to corruption and abuse. Despite the rapid assistance required to enforce an agreement and stabilize the country, coordination strategies are essential to avoid doing further harm. Effective donor coordination, meanwhile, can enhance the peace agreement provisions by accelerating their implementation and reach.

Local ownership. Donor participation in implementing the peace agreement needs to be tempered by judiciously involving and promoting local stakeholders. Their buy-in and active participation in implementing the agreement's provisions will help to sustain the peace after donors have left.

A flawed or incomplete negotiation or implementation process can set the stage for renewed conflict. Thus, dealing effectively with integrity issues and future governance practices is essential. If the public can begin to enjoy civil and legal rights, if people can begin to receive the quality public services from their government that they are entitled to as citizens, and if the basic framework for the rule of law is reestablished, formerly conflict-ridden countries have a chance to launch a stable peace. The conditions and strategies for negotiating and implementing peace with integrity are known and accessible. It is up to local stakeholders and other interested parties to catalyze these processes, find creative solutions through compromise and consensus, and pledge to implement their agreements in good faith.

It is a difficult and long-term task to transform a corrupt society. Peace agreements offer the possibility for a new beginning, including opportunities to strengthen good governance approaches and anticorruption controls. If the old corrupt elite are part of the negotiation process, are they up to this task? Can they be convinced to make the changes and institute the innovations needed to truly implement the transformation? History demonstrates that it is feasible given the right amount of pressure, incentives, political will, creativity, resources and interventions. The potential results are worth the effort.

Annex 1

Additional Case Study Sources

Burundi

International Crisis Group. "Burundi: Democracy and Peace at Risk." Africa Report no. 120, International Crisis Group, Brussels, November 30, 2006.

International Crisis Group. "Burundi: Finalizing Peace with the FNL." Africa Report no. 131, International Crisis Group, Brussels, August 28, 2007.

International Foundation for Electoral Systems. "Burundi Programs." 2008. http://www.ifes.org/burundi.html (accessed October 20, 2010).

Khadiagala, Gilbert. *Meddlers or Mediators? African Interveners in Civil Conflicts in Eastern Africa.* Leiden: Martinus Nijhoff Publishers, 2007.

World Bank Institute. "Burundi Governance Diagnostics." 2008. http://web.worldbank.org/WBSITE/EXTERNAL/WBI/EXTWBIGOVAN TCOR/0,,contentMDK:21402604~pagePK:64168445~piPK:64168309 ~theSitePK:1740530,00.html (accessed October 20, 2010).

United States Agency for International Development (USAID). "Burundi Annual Report FY 2005." Washington, DC: USAID, 2005. http://pdf.usaid.gov/pdf_docs/Pdacd858.pdf (accessed October 20, 2010).

El Salvador

Arnson, Cynthia, ed. *El Salvador's Democratic Transition Ten Years after the Peace Accord.* Reports on the Americas no. 6. Washington, DC: Woodrow Wilson International Center for Scholars, Latin America Program, 2003.

Cañas, Antonio, and Héctor Dada. "Political Transition and Institutionalization in El Salvador." In Cynthia Arnson, ed., *Comparative Peace Processes in Latin America.* Washington, DC: Woodrow Wilson Center Press, 1999.

Juhn, Tricia. *Negotiating Peace in El Salvador.* New York: St. Martin's Press, 1998.

Karl, Terry Lynn. "El Salvador's Negotiated Revolution." *Foreign Affairs* 71, no. 2 (Spring 1992), 147–164.

Mason, T. David. "The Civil War in El Salvador: A Retrospective Analysis." *Latin American Research Review* 34, no. 3 (1999): 179–196.

Saldaca, Nelson. "The Process of Negotiation in El Salvador." In James Zackrison, ed., *Crisis? What Crisis? Security Issues in Colombia.* Washington, DC: Institute for National Strategic Studies, National Defense University, 1999.

Transparency International. *El Salvador Country Report.* Berlin: Transparency International, 2003.

United Nations, Department of Public Information. "Secretary-General Says El Salvador Peace Accord Is Crowning Achievement of Long and Arduous Journey." Press Release, SG/SM/4685, CA/61, January 16, 1992.

Guatemala

Azpuru, Dinorah. "Peace and Democratization in Guatemala: Two Parallel Processes." In Cynthia Arnson, ed., *Comparative Peace Processes in Latin America.* Washington, DC: Woodrow Wilson Center Press, 1999.

Costello, Patrick. "Historical Background." *Accord* 2 (1997), 10–17.

Global Integrity. *Global Integrity Report 2004: Guatemala.* Washington, DC: Global Integrity, 2004. www.globalintegrity.org (accessed October 20, 2010).

Global Integrity. *Global Integrity Report 2006: Guatemala.* Washington, DC: Global Integrity, 2006. www.globalintegrity.org (accessed October 20, 2010).

Jonas, Susanne. *Of Centaurs and Doves: Guatemala's Peace Process.* Boulder, CO: Westview Press, 2000.

Molina, Otto Perez. "The Peace Process in Guatemala." In James Zackrison, ed., *Crisis? What Crisis? Security Issues in Colombia.* Washington, DC: Institute for National Strategic Studies, National Defense University, 1999.

Prado, Tania Palencia. "Advocates and Guarantors: Establishing Participative Democracy in Post-War Guatemala." *Accord* 2 (1997) 28–35.

Rosenthal, Gert. "The Peace Process in Guatemala and the Role of Third Parties." *International Journal on Minority and Group Rights* 8, no. 1 (2001): 55–59.

Salvesen, Hilde. *Guatemala: Five Years After the Peace Accords: The Challenges of Implementing Peace.* Oslo: International Peace Research Institute (PRIO), 2002.

Stanley, William, and David Holiday. "Broad Participation, Diffuse Responsibility: Peace Implementation in Guatemala." In Stephen Stedman, Donald Rothchild, and Elizabeth Cousens, eds., *Ending Civil Wars: The Implementation of Peace Agreements.* Boulder, CO: Lynne Rienner Publishers, 2002.

United States Agency for International Development (USAID). "USAID/Guatemala Programs." Washington, DC: USAID 2008. http://www.usaid.gov/gt/docs/web_page_version_programs_chart.pdf (accessed October 20, 2010).

Liberia

Adebajo, Adekeye. *Building Peace in West Africa.* Boulder, CO: Lynne Rienner Publishers, 2002.

Dodd, David and Eric Nelson. "Special Evaluation: USAID Activities under GEMAP in Liberia. PD-ACL-945 (July)." USAID Mission to Liberia, July 2008. http://pdf.usaid.gov/pdf_docs/PDACL945.pdf (accessed October 20, 2010).

Fayemi, J. Kayode. "Governing Insecurity in Post-Conflict States: The Case of Sierra Leone and Liberia." In Alan Bryden and Heiner Hänggi, eds., *Reform and Reconstruction of the Security Sector.* Berlin: LIT Verlag, 2004.

Fisher-Thompson, Jim. "U.S. Diplomat Sees Regional Action Key to Liberian Peace Process: Bruce Ehrnman Describes Africa 'Ownership' of Process," Washington, DC: US Department of State, September 15, 2003. http://www.globalsecurity.org/military/library/news/2003/09/mil-030915-usia03.htm (accessed October 20, 2010).

GEMAP program website, 2008. Available at http://www.gemap-liberia. org/success_stories.html (accessed November 2010).

Global Integrity. *Global Integrity Report 2006: Liberia.* Washington, DC: Global Integrity, 2006. www.globalintegrity.org (accessed October 20, 2010).

Hayner, Priscilla. "Negotiating Peace in Liberia: Preserving the Possibility for Justice." Geneva, Henry Dunant Centre for Humanitarian Dialogue: 2007.

Papua New Guinea

Asian Development Bank (ADB) and Organization for Economic Cooperation and Development (OECD). "Supporting the Fight against Corruption in Asia and the Pacific: The ADB/OECD Anti-Corruption Initiative." OECD, Paris, 2008. http://www.oecd.org/pages/0,3417,en_349 82156_34982385_1_1_1_1_1,00.html (accessed October 20, 2010).

Australian Government. "Bougainville Peace Process." Department of Foreign Affairs and Trade, Canberra, 2007. http://www.dfat.gov.au/geo/png/bougainville_peace_process.html (accessed October 20, 2010).

European Union. "European Union's Strategy in the Pacific: Forward in Partnership—Strategic Areas of Intervention for the European Union in Papua New Guinea." 2007. http://www.delpng.ec.europa.eu/docs/EU_booklet_07.pdf (accessed November 2010).

O'Callaghan, Mary-Louise. "The Origins of the Conflict." *Accord* 12 (2002), 6–11.

Organization for Economic Cooperation and Development (OECD). "Gender, Institutions and Development Database 2009." OECD, Paris, 2008. http://stats.oecd.org/Index.aspx?DatasetCode=GID2 (accessed in November 2010).

Regan, Anthony. "The Bougainville Political Settlement and the Prospects for Sustainable Peace." *Pacific Economic Bulletin* 17, no. 1 (May 2002), 114–129.

Regan, Anthony. "Phases of the Negotiation Process." *Accord* 12 (2002), 32–35.

Regan, Anthony. "Lessons from a Successful Peace Process in Bougainville, Papua New Guinea, 1997–2005." Senior Fellow Project Report, United States Institute of Peace, Washington, DC, 2005.

Regan, Anthony. "External versus Internal Incentives in Peace Processes: The Bougainville Experience," *Accord* 19 (2008): 44–49.

Transparency International. *National Integrity Report: Papua New Guinea.* Berlin: Transparency International, 2003.

Wolfers, Edward. "Joint Creation: The Bougainville Peace Agreement—and Beyond." *Accord* 12 (2002): 44–49.

Sierra Leone

Accountability Alert. "UNDP Supports Ministry Of Finance and Economic Development to Enhance Transparency, Accountability and Participation (CAP) in The National Budget Process in Sierra Leone." 2008. http://news.sl/drwebsite/publish/article_20057619.shtml (accessed September 2008).

Adebajo, Adekeye. *Building Peace in West Africa*. Boulder, CO: Lynne Rienner Publishers, 2002.

Bright, Dennis. "Implementing the Lomé Peace Agreement." *Accord* 9 (September 2000): 36–41.

Department for International Development. *Annual Review of DFID Support to Anticorruption Commission Phase 2*. 2006. http://www.dfid.gov.uk/pubs/files/anticorruption-sierraleone.pdf (accessed November 2010).

Francis, David J. "Torturous Path to Peace: The Lomé Accord and Postwar Peacebuilding in Sierra Leone." *Security Dialogue* 31, no. 3 (September 2000): 360.

Gberie, Lansana. "First Stages on the Road to Peace: The Abidjan Process (1995–96)." Conciliation Resources, London, 2000. http://www.c-r.org/our-work/accord/sierra-leone/first-stages.php (accessed October 20, 2010).

Gberie, Lansana. "War and Peace in Sierra Leone: Diamonds, Corruption and the Lebanese Connection." Occasional Paper no. 6, The Diamonds and Human Security Project, Partnership Africa Canada, Ottawa, November 2002.

Global Integrity Report. "Sierra Leone." 2008. http://www.globalintegrity.org/reports/2006/SIERRA%20LEONE/scorecard.cfm?subcategoryID=102&countryID=33 (accessed August 8, 2008).

Hanlon, Joseph. "Is the International Community Helping to Recreate the Preconditions for War in Sierra Leone?" *The Round Table* 94, no. 381 (September 2005): 459–472.

Hayner, Priscilla. "Negotiating Peace in Liberia: Preserving the Possibility for Justice." Henry Dunant Centre for Humanitarian Dialogue, Geneva, 2007.

International Crisis Group. *Sierra Leone: The State of Security and Governance.* Africa Report no. 67, Freetown and Brussels, September 2, 2003.

Rashid, Ismail. "The Lomé Peace Negotiations." *Accord* 9 (September 2000): 26–33.

Transparency International. *National Integrity Study: Sierra Leone.* Berlin: Transparency International, 2004.

ANNEX 2

Peace Provisions Related to Anticorruption and Good Governance Issues

T he following excerpts from peace agreements concluded for El Salvador, Guatemala, Sierra Leone, Burundi, Papua New Guinea, and Liberia highlight the anticorruption and good governance provisions that were negotiated to resolve some of the major underlying causes of the internal conflicts in those countries.

El Salvador
Peace Agreement between the government of El Salvador and the Frente Farabundo Martí para la Liberación Nacional (FMLN) (January 16, 1992)

End to impunity. The Parties recognize the need to clarify and put an end to any indication of impunity on the part of officers of the armed forces, particularly in cases where respect for human rights is jeopardized. To that end, the Parties refer this issue to the Commission on the Truth for consideration and resolution. All of this shall be without prejudice to the principle, which the Parties also recognize, that acts of this nature, regardless of the sector to which their perpetrators belong, must be the object of exemplary action by the law courts so that the punishment prescribed by law is meted out to those found responsible.

Public security forces. Under the constitutional reform resulting from the Mexico Agreements, the safeguarding of peace, tranquility, order and public security in both urban and rural areas shall be the responsibility of the National Civil Police, which shall be under the control of civilian authorities. The National Civil Police and the armed forces shall be independent and shall be placed under the authority of different ministries.

National Civil Police. Members of the National Civil Police shall not commit any act of corruption. They shall also strongly oppose such acts and shall combat them.

Judicial Training School. ... [T]he Judicial Training School ... [will operate] under the responsibility of the National Judicial Council, whose purpose will be to ensure the continued improvement of training professional judges and other judicial officials, as well as that of members of the Attorney General of the Republic, to investigate the country's judicial problems and promote solutions to the same, and to foster greater ties of solidarity among them and consistency in an overview on the judiciary in a democratic state.

Attorney for the Defense of National Human Rights. The National Counsel for the Defense of Human Rights shall be appointed within ninety days after entry into force of the constitutional reform emanating from the Mexico agreements.... The [implementing] bill will establish appropriate means to enforce the strong commitment by the parties during negotiations to identify and eradicate any groups practicing systematic violations of human rights, including arbitrary detention, abductions and adjustment and other forms of attack against freedom, integrity and security of person, which includes a commitment to identify and, where necessary, eliminate and dismantle any prison or place of detention. In any event, the Parties agree to give top priority to the investigation of cases of this nature, under the verification of ONUSAL.

Electoral System. The Parties reaffirm their commitment, contained in the Mexico agreements, to promote a comprehensive project to reform the electoral system. To this end, they seek to appoint COPAZ UNSCOM designed for that purpose in the Mexico agreements. The Commission will review the draft Electoral Code reforms submitted to the Legislature by the Central Election Board and the contributions to their members or independent experts who are invited for this purpose. The Special Commission shall organize its work so that it could be exploited within the time provided to reform the electoral system.

Guatemala
Peace Agreement (December 29, 1996)

Agreement on a Firm and Lasting Peace. The constitutional reforms set out in the Peace Agreements provide the fundamental substantive basis for the reconciliation of Guatemalan society within the framework of the rule of law, democratic coexistence and the full observance of and strict respect for human rights.

Administration of justice. The integrity and efficiency of the judicial function fulfills the task of guaranteeing the rules of social relations, a guarantee which can become operative only if there is security, as manifested in the substantive rights prescribed by law, the fair settlement of disputes, universal respect for procedural norms, the punishment of offenders and reparation for injury.

That is why it is important to strengthen the judicial function so that, within the constitutional framework that provides general guarantees for the administration of justice, free access to the administration of justice, regardless of financial means, can become a reality, based, in particular, on the multi-ethnic, multicultural and multilingual nature of Guatemala; the impartiality and independence of judges; the reasonable and prompt resolution of social conflicts; the provision of alternative mechanisms for resolving such conflicts; and a career judicial service which strives to ensure the professional excellence of judges, as well as proper recognition of the dignity of their profession and of their rights and responsibilities with regard to training and advanced training, without prejudice to a disciplinary system which, while respecting the rights of defence and due process, guarantees the proper exercise of the judicial function, with the power to impose penalties being exercised solely by the judiciary.

Electoral Reform Commission. Recognizing the role of the Supreme Electoral Tribunal in safeguarding and strengthening the electoral regime, the Parties agree to request the Tribunal, through this Agreement, to establish and preside over an Electoral Reform Commission charged with publishing a report and making a series of recommendations on electoral reform and the corresponding legislative amendments.

Transparency and Publicity. In order to promote greater transparency in the presentation of candidates by assemblies of political parties, action should be taken to ensure that all party members are informed of the convocation and holding of the general assemblies of political parties. The Electoral Reform Commission could examine whether compliance in convoking and holding the assemblies of political parties might be verified as a matter of routine by the National Registry or whether it would be useful to amend the law to enable the Supreme Electoral Tribunal to supervise effectively the convocation and holding of assemblies of political parties, as well as their results.

In order to ensure transparency in the financing of election campaigns and that voter preference is not supplanted by spending power, the Parties consider that the Supreme Electoral Tribunal should have the power to set a ceiling for campaign spending by each presidential candidate in the mass media. It is recommended that consideration be given to the possibility of providing and facilitating the use of media time and space free of charge for all parties on an equal footing.

Parties and candidates should be compelled to make available such accounting records and reports as may be required from them by the National Registry in order to verify that their sources of funding are lawful. The calculation of campaign spending should include, at market prices, any advertising donated to the parties during the election campaign.

It would also be useful to promote a reform of the Penal Code to characterize the acceptance of illicit campaign funding as a crime, establishing that anyone who receives or authorizes the receipt of such contributions for the funding of political organizations or election campaigns is guilty of such a crime. The reform would establish the corresponding criminal penalties.

Public Information Campaigns. The increasingly active participation of citizens in the electoral process is a guarantee of the legitimacy and representativeness of the elected authorities. This objective would be more easily achieved if ongoing campaigns to educate, motivate and inform citizens were carried out. The Electoral Reform Commission would examine the possibility of conducting information campaigns to:

(a) Explain the importance of the right of citizens to vote and to be elected;

(b) Encourage and promote the timely preparation of electoral rolls;

(c) Provide information on how to vote, the documents to be presented at voting tables and centres and the hours during which voting takes place;

(d) Provide information on how to organize civic committees or join a political party.

Participation and Consensus-Building. Expanded social participation is a bulwark against corruption, privilege, distortions of development and the abuse of economic and political power to the detriment of society. Therefore, it is an instrument for the eradication of economic, social and political polarization in society.

In addition to representing a factor in democratization, citizen participation in economic and social development is essential in order to promote productivity and economic growth, achieve a more equitable distribution of wealth and train human resources. It ensures transparency in public policies and their orientation towards the common good rather than special interests, the effective protection of the interests of the most vulnerable groups, efficiency in providing services and, consequently, the integral development of the individual.

Modernization of Government Services. Government services should become an efficient tool of development policies. To this end, the Government undertakes to:

(a) Deepen the decentralization and redistribution of the powers, responsibilities and resources concentrated in the central Government in order to modernize, render effective and streamline government services. Decentralization should ensure the transfer of decision-making power and sufficient resources to the appropriate levels (local, municipal, departmental and regional) so as to meet the needs of socio-economic development in an efficient way and promote close cooperation between government bodies and the population. This implies:

(i) Promoting an amendment to the Executive Authority Act and the Departmental Control and Administration Act and, in particular, to Decree No. 586 of 1956, which will make it possible to simplify, decentralize and redistribute government services;

(ii) Promoting the decentralization of support systems, including the purchasing and procurement system, the human resources system, the information-gathering and statistical system and the financial management system.

(b) Reform, strengthen and modernize the Comptroller's Office.

Professionalization and Advancement of Public Servants. The State should have a skilled labour force which can ensure the honest and efficient management of public funds. To this end, it is necessary to: (a) Establish a career civil service; (b) Adopt legal and administrative measures to ensure real compliance with the Integrity and Accountability Act; (c) Promote criminal sanctions for acts of corruption and misappropriation of public funds.

Legislative Branch. Legislative authority belongs to the Guatemalan Congress, which is composed of deputies elected directly by universal and secret vote. It has a fundamental role to play in the representation of Guatemalan society, since democracy requires a body in which the overall situation of the country is embodied in an institutional form, harmoniously integrating a variety of interests.

For the legitimacy of the legislative body to be strengthened, it must fully discharge the following duties:

(a) The legislative function, in the interest of the people of Guatemala;

(b) Public discussion of essential national issues;

(c) Representation of the people;

(d) Its responsibilities towards the other branches of the State.

The Parties agree that the legislative branch must be enhanced, modernized and reinforced, and that the Presidency of the Congress will be requested to set up a multiparty agency for that purpose. This agency will work in conjunction with those legislative commissions which have been entrusted with responsibilities in connection with the follow-up to the agreements on a firm and lasting peace and the process of modernization and strengthening of the Congress of the Republic. Its agenda, minimal and open-ended, will give priority to the following aspects:

(a) Revision of the Act on the Rules of Procedure of the Congress, in order to streamline parliamentary work and enable the Guatemalan Congress as a branch of the State to carry out what is required of it by the Political Constitution and by public opinion, and to enhance efficiency in the initiation, discussion and adoption stages of the legislative process;

(b) Proper utilization of constitutional mechanisms for the supervision of the executive branch, to ensure clarity in government policy, consistency in its programmes, transparency in the planning and implementation of the State budget, examination and evaluation of the responsibility of ministers and other high-ranking officials for their administrative acts or omissions, and monitoring of government administration to protect the general interests of the population while preserving institutional legitimacy;

(c) Appropriate legislative measures to strengthen the administration of justice.

System of Justice. One of the major structural weaknesses of the Guatemalan State stems from the system of administration of justice, which is one of the key public services. This system and the functioning of judicial proceedings within it suffer from faults and deficiencies. The antiquated legal practices, slow proceedings, absence of modern office management systems and lack of supervision of officials and employees of the judicial branch breed corruption and inefficiency.

The reform and modernization of the administration of justice should be geared to preventing the judiciary from producing or covering up a system of impunity and corruption. The judicial process is not a simple procedure regulated by codes and ordinary laws but rather an instrument for ensuring the basic right to justice, which is manifested in a guarantee of impartiality, objectivity, universality and equality before the law.

A priority in this respect is to reform the administration of justice in order to put an end to inefficiency, eradicate corruption and guarantee free access to the justice system, impartiality in the application of the law, judicial independence, ethical authority and the integrity and modernization of the system as a whole.

The Judiciary. Article 203: the article should contain an initial reference to guarantees of the administration of justice and, as such, include: free access to the system of justice in the person's own language; respect for the multi-ethnic, multicultural and multilingual nature of Guatemala; legal assistance to those who cannot afford their own counsel; the impartiality and independence of judges; reasonable and prompt resolution of social conflicts and provision of alternative conflict-resolution mechanisms.

Penal Code. Institute a reform of the Penal Code that gives priority to the criminal prosecution of those offences that are most detrimental to society, takes into account the country's cultural differences and customs, fully protects human rights and characterizes threats and coercion of judicial personnel, bribery, graft and corruption as particularly serious offences which are severely punished.

Professional excellence. Devise a system for the selection and appointment of appeals court magistrates through competitive examinations;... Strengthen the Judicial Training School and the training unit of the Public Prosecutor's Office as the main bodies for the selection and further training of judges, magistrates and prosecutors.

National Civil Police. The protection of life and the security of the citizens, the maintenance of public order, the prevention and investigation of crime and the swift and transparent administration of justice cannot be guaranteed without the appropriate structuring of the public security forces. The design of a new model and its implementation are fundamental aspects of the strengthening of civilian power.

Professionalization of civil servants. Article 136 of the Constitution stipulates that the right of Guatemalan citizens to seek public office must be guaranteed. However, only individuals with ability, honesty and integrity are eligible to do so. Accordingly, pursuant to the Agreement on Social and Economic Aspects and Agrarian Situation, the Government shall accord priority to the following activities:

(a) Modernization of government services, including publication of personnel selection and classification procedures for all departments of the executive branch, and review of the staffing table to ensure that employees and officials meet the criteria of honesty and ability;

(b) Establishment of a career civil service;

(c) Promotion of the effective implementation of legislation on integrity and accountability;

(d) Strengthening and modernization of the Comptroller's Office;

(e) Promotion of criminal sanctions for acts of corruption and misappropriation of public funds.

Sierra Leone
Peace Agreement between the government of Sierra Leone and the Revolutionary United Front of Sierra Leone (July 7, 1999)

Committed to promoting popular participation in the governance of the country and the advancement of democracy in a socio-political framework free of inequality, nepotism and corruption.

Governance. The Government of Sierra Leone and the RUF/SL, recognizing the right of the people of Sierra Leone to live in peace, and desirous of finding a transitional mechanism to incorporate the RUF/SL into governance within the spirit and letter of the Constitution, agree to the following formulas for structuring the government for the duration of the period before the next elections, as prescribed by the Constitution, managing scarce public resources for the benefit of the development of the people of Sierra Leone and sharing the responsibility of implementing the peace. Each of these formulas (not in priority order) is contained in a separate Article of this Part of the present Agreement; and may be further detailed in protocols annexed to it.

Commission for the Consolidation of Peace. A Commission for the Consolidation of Peace (hereinafter termed the CCP), shall be established within two weeks of the signing of the present Agreement to implement a post-conflict programme that ensures reconciliation and the welfare of all parties to the conflict, especially the victims of war. The CCP shall have the overall goal and responsibility for supervising and monitoring the implementation of and compliance with the provisions of the present Agreement relative to the promotion of national reconciliation and the consolidation of peace.

Commission for the Management of Strategic Resources, National Reconstruction and Development. Given the emergency situation facing the country, the parties agree that the Government shall exercise full control over the exploitation of gold, diamonds and other resources, for the benefit of the people of Sierra Leone. Accordingly, a Commission for the Management of Strategic Resources, National Reconstruction and Development (hereinafter termed the CMRRD) shall be established and charged with the responsibility of securing and monitoring the legitimate exploitation of Sierra Leone's gold and diamonds, and other resources that are determined to be of strategic importance for national security and welfare as well as cater for post-war rehabilitation and reconstruction, as provided for under Article XXVIII of the present Agreement. . . .

The CMRRD shall ensure, through the appropriate authorities, the security of the areas covered under this Article, and shall take all necessary measures against unauthorized exploitation. . . .

The proceeds from the transactions of gold and diamonds shall be public monies which shall enter a special Treasury account to be spent exclusively on the development of the people of Sierra Leone, with appropriations for public education, public health, infrastructural development, and compensation for incapacitated war victims as well as post-war rehabilitation and reconstruction. Priority spending shall go to rural areas. . . .

All agreements and transactions referred to in this Article shall be subject to full public disclosure and records of all correspondence, negotiations, business transactions and any other matters related to exploitation, management, local or international marketing, and any other matter shall be public documents.

The Commission shall issue monthly reports, including the details of all the transactions related to gold and diamonds, and other licenses or concessions of natural resources, and its own administrative costs.

The Government commits itself to propose and support an amendment to the Constitution to make the exploitation of gold and diamonds the legitimate domain of the people of Sierra Leone, and to determine that the proceeds be used for the development of Sierra Leone, particularly public education, public health, infrastructure development, and compensation of incapacitated war victims as well as post-war reconstruction and development.

National Electoral Commission. A new independent National Electoral Commission (hereinafter termed the NEC) shall be set up by the Government, not later than three months after the signing of the present Agreement.

Guarantee and Promotion of Human Rights. The basic civil and political liberties recognized by the Sierra Leone legal system and contained in the declarations and principles of Human Rights adopted by the UN and OAU, especially the Universal Declaration of Human Rights and the African Charter on Human and People's Rights, shall be fully protected and promoted within Sierra Leonean society.

These include the right to life and liberty, freedom from torture, the right to a fair trial, freedom of conscience, expression and association, and the right to take part in the governance of one's country.

Human Rights Violations. A Truth and Reconciliation Commission shall be established to address impunity, break the cycle of violence, provide a forum for both the victims and perpetrators of human rights violations to tell their story, [and] get a clear picture of the past in order to facilitate genuine healing and reconciliation.

Burundi
The Arusha Agreement (August 28, 2000)

[Establish institutions] of a new political, economic, social and judicial order in Burundi, in the context of a new constitution inspired by Burundian realities and founded on the values of justice, the rule of law, democracy, good governance, pluralism, respect for the fundamental rights and freedoms of the individual, unity, solidarity, equality between women and men, mutual understanding and tolerance among the various political and ethnic components of the Burundian people.

Principles and measures relating to public administration. A qualified, efficient and responsible administration that shall work in the general interest and promote balance, including gender balance. A transparent administration committed to the sound management of public affairs. Training, in such a way as to include all the components of Burundian society, of civil servants, particularly for regional and local government, by establishing a national school of administration. Equal opportunities of access to this sector for all men and women through strict respect for, or the introduction of, laws and regulations governing the recruitment of State personnel and the staff of public and parastatal enterprises, as well as through transparency of competitive entrance examinations. Depoliticization of the public administration to ensure its stability; in this respect, there is a need for legislation that will distinguish between political and technical functions; staff in the first category may change with the Government, whereas the technical staff must be guaranteed continuity.

Principles and measures relating to education. Transparency and fairness in non-competitive and competitive examinations.

Principles and measures relating to justice. Pursuant to the relevant provisions of Protocol II to the Agreement:

a. Promotion of impartial and independent justice. In this respect, all petitions and appeals relating to assassinations and political trials shall be made through the National Truth and Reconciliation Commission...;
b. Reform of the judicial machinery at all levels, *inter alia* with a view to correcting ethnic and gender imbalances where they exist;
c. Amendment of laws where necessary (Criminal Code, Code of Criminal Procedure, Civil Code, Nationality Act, etc.);
d. Reform of the Judicial Service Commission so as to ensure its independence and that of the judicial system;
e. Organization of a judicial training programme, *inter alia* through the establishment of a National School for the Magistracy;
f. Provision of adequate human and material resources for the courts;
g. Establishment of the post of Ombudsperson.

Principles and measures relating to the economy. Legislation and structures for combating financial crime and corruption (tax legislation, customs legislation, legislation on public markets, etc.). Recovery of State property plundered by some citizens. Introduction of incentives for economic development in the context of fairness and harmony.

Democracy and Good Governance. We, the Parties, aware of the vital need to promote lasting peace in Burundi and to put an end to the conflict, division and suffering inflicted on the Burundian people,

Reaffirming our commitment to a democratic system of government, inspired by the realities of our country, that guarantees security and justice for all, and is founded on the values of unity without exclusion,

Have agreed: To ensure that a constitutional text for the people of Burundi is drafted during the transition period that is in conformity with the principles set forth in Chapter I of the present Protocol, and to ensure that such a text is adopted and brought into force in accordance with the timeframes and procedures herein, in conformity with a vision of democracy and good governance and the principles listed hereunder.

Constitutional Principles of the Post-Transition Constitution
1. All Burundians are equal in value and dignity. All citizens are entitled to equal rights and to equal protection of the law. No Burundian shall be excluded from the social, economic or political life of the nation on account of her/his race, language, religion, gender, or ethnic origin.
2. All Burundians are entitled to live in Burundi in security and peace, and must live in harmony with one another while respecting one another's dignity and tolerating one another's differences.
3. Government shall be based on the will of the Burundian people, shall be accountable to them, and shall respect their fundamental rights and freedoms.
4. The Government of Burundi shall be so structured as to ensure that all Burundians are represented in and by it; that there is equal opportunity to serve in it; that all citizens have access to government services; and that the decisions and actions of government enjoy the widest possible level of support.
5. The task of government shall be to realize the aspirations of the Burundian people, and in particular to heal the divisions of the past, to improve the quality of life of all Burundians, and to ensure that all Burundians are able to live in Burundi free from fear, discrimination, disease and hunger.
6. The function of the political system shall be to unite, reassure and reconcile all Burundians while ensuring that the Government is able to serve the people of Burundi, who are its source of power and authority. In its functioning, the Government shall respect the separation of powers, the rule of law, and the principles of good governance and transparency in the management of public affairs.

Political parties. For the purposes of promoting democracy, a national law may authorize the financing of political parties on an equitable basis in proportion to the number of seats they hold in the National Assembly. Such financing may apply both to the functioning of the political parties and to electoral campaigns, and shall be transparent. The law shall define the types of subsidies, benefits and facilities that the State may grant political parties.

The Legislature. The National Assembly shall pass legislation, oversee the actions of the Government and exercise all other functions assigned to it by the Constitution. The National Assembly shall be responsible for approving the national budget. This provision shall not preclude the submission of matters for popular approval by way of referendum.

A Court of Audit responsible for examining and certifying the accounts of all public services shall be established and organized by law. Its composition shall be specified in the post-transition Constitution. It shall be given the resources required for the performance of its duties. Administrative departments shall not withhold their co-operation from the Court of Audit. The Court of Audit shall submit to the National Assembly a report on the regularity of the general account of the State, and shall also ascertain whether public funds have been spent in accordance with the proper procedures and in accordance with the budget approved by the National Assembly.

The Executive. The President of the Republic may be impeached for serious misconduct, impropriety or corruption by resolution of two-thirds of the members of the National Assembly and the Senate sitting together.

The Supreme Court shall receive a written statement of the assets and property of the President, the Vice-Presidents and members of the Government when they assume and relinquish office.

Local government. The law shall make provision for the circumstances under which a commune administrator may be dismissed or suspended, by the central authorities or by the Commune Council, for good cause including incompetence, corruption, gross misconduct or embezzlement.

The Judiciary. The judicial authority of the Republic of Burundi shall be vested in the courts. The Judiciary shall be impartial and independent and shall be governed solely by the Constitution and the law. No person may interfere with the Judiciary in the performance of its judicial functions. The President of the Court of Appeal, the presidents of the High Courts, the public prosecutors and the state counsels shall be appointed by the President of the Republic following nomination by the Judicial Service Commission and confirmation by the Senate.

The Judicial Service Commission shall have a secretariat. It shall be chaired by the President of the Republic, assisted by the Minister of Justice. It shall meet on an *ad hoc* basis. Its members who are not members of the Judiciary shall not be construed as members of the Judiciary solely because they are members of this oversight commission.

The Judicial Service Commission shall be the highest disciplinary body of the magistracy. It shall hear complaints by individuals, or by the Ombudsperson, against the professional conduct of magistrates, as well as appeals against disciplinary measures and grievances concerning the career of magistrates. No magistrate may be dismissed other than for professional misconduct or incompetence, and solely on the basis of a finding by the Judicial Service Commission.

The administration. The administration shall function in accordance with the democratic values and principles enshrined in the Constitution, and with the law. The administration shall be so structured, and all civil servants shall so perform their duties, as to serve all users of public services with efficiency, courtesy, impartiality and equity. Embezzlement, corruption, extortion and misappropriation of all kinds shall be punishable in accordance with the law. Any state employee convicted of corruption shall be dismissed from the public administration following a disciplinary inquiry.

An independent Ombudsperson shall be created by the Constitution. The organization and functioning of her/his service shall be determined by law. The Ombudsperson shall hear complaints and conduct inquiries relating to mismanagement and infringements of citizens' rights committed by members of the public administration and the judiciary, and shall make recommendations thereon to the appropriate authorities. She/he shall also mediate between the administration and citizens and between administrative departments, and shall act as an observer of the functioning of the public administration. The Ombudsperson shall possess the powers and resources required to perform her/his duty. She/he shall report annually to the National Assembly and the Senate. Her/his report shall be published in the Official Gazette of Burundi. The Ombudsperson shall be appointed by the National Assembly by a three-quarters majority. The appointment shall be subject to confirmation by the Senate.

Judicial and administrative reforms. For purposes of improving the judicial services in Burundi, the transitional Government shall implement the following reforms:

Steps shall be taken to discourage corruption, to denounce officials guilty of corruption, to enforce all legislation related to corruption, to establish effective oversight bodies, to improve working conditions in the judicial sector and to take necessary measures to require civil servants to report instances of corruption;

Elections. The [Electoral] Commission shall have as its functions: … To ensure that these elections are free, fair and transparent.

For purposes of the first election, each Commune Council shall appoint a Commune Administrator and may dismiss her/him for good cause, including incompetence, corruption, misconduct or embezzlement. For subsequent elections, the National Assembly and the Senate may, after evaluation, legislate for the administrators to be elected by direct universal suffrage.

Papua New Guinea
Bougainville Peace Agreement (August 30, 2001)

Objectives of Autonomy. On the basis of shared acceptance of the sovereignty of Papua New Guinea, the agreed autonomy arrangements are intended to:

a. facilitate the expression and development of Bougainville identity and the relationship between Bougainville and the rest of Papua New Guinea;
b. empower Bougainvilleans to solve their own problems, manage their own affairs and work to realize their aspirations within the framework of the Papua New Guinea Constitution;
c. promote the unity of Papua New Guinea;
d. provide for a democratic and accountable system of government for Bougainville that meets internationally accepted standards of good governance, including protection of human rights.

Principles and Standards for Development and Contents of Constitution. Subject to other provisions of this Agreement, the arrangements used to establish the Bougainville Constitution and the structures and procedures for the autonomous Bougainville Government established under it will meet internationally accepted standards of good governance.

Accountability of Government Institutions. The Bougainville Constitution will make provision for the accountability of all institutions created under it….Provision in relation to accountability will include arrangements concerning a public accounts committee of the legislature, audit of provincial accounts and management of the revenue funds and accounts of the autonomous Bougainville Government.

Fiscal Accountability. The National Constitution will set out the requirements within which the Bougainville Constitution will establish a framework for orderly management of the autonomous Bougainville Government's financial and other resources. This framework will include requirements that the autonomous Bougainville Government will do the following in accordance with law:

a. raise revenues, including loans, and manage National Government grants;

b. approve and administer annual budgets (and, where appropriate, supplementary budgets), comprising estimates of revenue and expenditure, and appropriations for the main functions of government;

c. make expenditures;

d. maintain proper transparent and accurate accounts, compatible with international standards;

e. ensure that accounts are subject to regular audits additional to audits by the National Auditor-General (or his agents); and

f. provide for a public accounts committee in the Bougainville legislature, which shall receive, consider and make recommendations on auditors' reports.

Follow-Up to Audits. Should any audit carried out by the National Government pursuant to this agreement disclose systematic and widespread abuse (or misuse) of funding provided to the autonomous Bougainville Government by way of Recurrent or Conditional Grant then the following steps will take place:

a. the National Government will advise the autonomous Bougainville Government of the details of the abuse;

b. the autonomous Bougainville Government will immediately investigate the concerns raised by the National Government and will take appropriate steps to remedy the situation as soon as is reasonably possible;

c. should the autonomous Bougainville Government, after investigation, disagree with the National Government's concerns or if the National Government is not satisfied with the response of the Bougainville Government they will consult with each other to resolve the differences;

d. if the consultations do not resolve the matter the National Auditor General and the auditor responsible for auditing accounts on behalf of the autonomous Bougainville Government will consider the matters in question and provide a report making joint recommendations to resolve these matters;

e. the autonomous Bougainville Government will implement the reasonable joint recommendations of both auditors to their satisfaction;

f. if the autonomous Bougainville Government fails to attend to the recommendations within a reasonable time, the National Government may withhold the further release of funds (other than the costs of essential services, such as salaries and medical supplies) until such time as the recommendations have been attended to;

g. should the National Government or the autonomous Bougainville Government disagree on reasonable grounds as to the recommendations, or should there be a dispute as to whether the autonomous Bougainville Government has implemented the recommendations, recourse may be had to the agreed dispute resolution procedures.

Standards of good governance. The benchmarks to be used in determining good governance will take account of internationally accepted standards of good governance as they are applicable and implemented in the circumstances of Bougainville and the rest of Papua New Guinea. These benchmarks include democracy and opportunities for participation by Bougainvilleans, transparency, and accountability, as well as respect for human rights and the rule of law, including the Constitution of Papua New Guinea.

Liberia
Comprehensive Peace Agreement between the government of Liberia and the Liberians United for Reconciliation and Democracy (LURD) and the Movement for Democracy in Liberia (MODEL) and Political Parties (August 18, 2003)

Human Rights. These basic civil and political rights include the right to life and liberty, freedom from torture, the right to a fair trial, freedom of conscience, expression and association, and the right to take part in the governance of one's country.

Establishment of a Governance Reform Commission. A Governance Reform Commission is hereby established. The Commission shall be a vehicle for the promotion of the principles of good governance in Liberia. The mandate of the Commission shall be to:

- Review the existing program for the Promotion of Good Governance in Liberia, with the objective of adjusting its scope and strategy for implementation;
- Develop public sector management reforms through assessment, reforms, capacity building and performance monitoring;
- Ensure transparency and accountability in governance in all government institutions and activities, including acting as the Public Ombudsman;
- Ensure subsidiarity in governance through decentralisation and participation;
- Ensure a national and regional balance in appointments without compromising quality and integrity;
- Ensure an enabling environment which will attract private sector direct investment;
- Monitor, assess, and report to the National Transitional Legislative Assembly (NTLA) on the implementation and impact of activities undertaken to encourage the practice of good governance in Liberia.

The Structure of the Commission shall be as follows:

The Commission shall be established as an independent Commission with seven (7) permanent members appointed by the Chairman and confirmed by the NTLA, from a list provided by civil society organisations. It shall have a chairperson who must be from the civil society. Its membership shall include women.

The members must have experience in one or more of the following: Public Sector Management, Corporate Law, Finance and Auditing Regulations, Trade Policies and NGO activities. They must be men and women of known integrity with national and/or international experience.

Contract and Monopolies Commission (CMC). A Contract and Monopolies Commission is hereby established in Liberia to oversee activities of a contractual nature undertaken by the National Transitional Government of Liberia (NTGL). Its mandate shall include:

a. Ensuring that all public financial and budgetary commitments entered into by the NTGL are transparent, non-monopolistic and in accordance with the laws of Liberia and internationally accepted norms of commercial practice;
b. Ensuring that public officers will not use their positions to benefit from any contract financed from public funds;

c. Publishing all tenders in the media and on its own website to ensure maximum competition and transparency. The Commission shall also publish on its website the result of tenders as well as a record of all commercial entities that have participated and succeeded in reviewing contracts;

d. Ensuring the formulation and effective implementation of sound macro-economic policies that will support sustainable development goals;

e. Collaborate with the international institutions to provide finance to Liberia in carrying out its functions

The Commission shall consist of five (5) members appointed by the Chairman, on the approval of the NTLA, from the broad spectrum of civil society, who may or may not be technocrats. The members shall be persons of sound judgment and integrity who are independent of the commercial sector. The members must have sufficient experience to be able to review contract documents and procedures to ensure that public funds are used without favour and with complete transparency. The members of the CMC shall be assisted by independent national and international experts.

Electoral Reform. The Parties agree that the present electoral system in Liberia shall be reformed. In this regard and amongst other measures that may be undertaken, the National Elections Commission (NEC) shall be reconstituted and shall be independent. It shall operate in conformity with UN standards, in order to ensure that the rights and interests of Liberians are guaranteed, and that the elections are organized in a manner that is acceptable to all. Appointments to the NEC shall be made by the Chairman with the advice and consent of the NTLA within three months from the entry into force of this Agreement. It shall be composed of men and women of integrity.

ANNEX 3

Experiences of Development Assistance Projects that Support Anticorruption Provisions

Donor-sponsored development assistance projects in the postagreement period have produced a wide range of results in support of anticorruption and good governance reforms that were conceptualized in the peace agreements. Some of these projects and their effects—successes, failures, or somewhere in between—are described below.

El Salvador

Law Enforcement Program. USAID support to the National Civilian Police (PNC) was intended to build the capacity of local law enforcement by providing institutional and logistical support. In all, 1,596 police officials and 650 public prosecutors were trained and computers were provided to improve case investigations.

Result. The National Civilian Police Force and the National Public Security Academy are now well established. The police operate specialized investigative units successfully and the Inspector General's Office and Internal Affairs have become more efficient in investigating citizen complaints and disciplining officers. Law enforcement mechanisms are now more accessible to people. Overall, the El Salvador police reforms have been praised as a positive legacy of the peace accords. However, internal discipline in police units and the strength of investigative units are still questioned by many.
Source: Rubén Zamora with David Holiday, "The Struggle for Lasting Reform: Vetting Processes in El Salvador," in Alexander Mayer-Rieckh and Pablo de Greiff, eds., *Justice as Prevention: Vetting Public Employees in Transitional Societies* (New York: Social Science Research Council, 2007).

Decentralization Program. The Municipal Development/Citizen Participation project was funded by USAID to enhance citizen participation in local democratic processes and improve the capacity of local governance.

Results. The project increased local resources for urban services: Local government revenues increased over 30 percent during the project and important urban services (water and rural road maintenance) were decentralized. The local community was encouraged to get involved in local governance through participatory planning, budget hearings, and radio talk shows. The project also succeeded in developing local integrated financial management systems, automated billings and collection systems, commercial accounting packages for municipal services, and strengthened staff capacity to apply these systems. The success of the project is evident in the political motivation for further decentralization. However, encouraging citizen participation in local policy making has been a major challenge. *Source:* Stephen Pereira, "Case Study: El Salvador Post Conflict Program in Democracy and Governance," Research Triangle Institute, July 2003, http://www.rti.org/pubs/El_Salvador_Case_Study.pdf (accessed November 2010).

Guatemala

Judicial Reform Program. USAID has promoted a Rule of Law program to improve the transparency and efficiency of criminal judicial processes through expansion of oral procedures, support for justice centers, strengthened prosecution in corruption cases, and support for crime prevention. The program has initiated a twenty-four-hour court system to speed arraignments. The Central Case Management Center centralizes all case information, statistics, and clerk functions, and combines court, prosecutor, defender, and bail services in one location to enhance coordination and efficient case management.

Results. While it initially failed, the twenty-four-hour court initiative has achieved certain efficiencies since it received significant multi-institutional support. The number of cases dismissed due to lack of evidence has declined from 77 percent to under 15 percent. Nearly 50 percent of cases were given alternatives to detention, such as bail, house arrest, weekly presentations in local court, or restrictions on travel. In 35 percent of cases, the judge ruled for preventative detention. Within the first three months of the court's initiation, drug consumption cases dropped from over 30 percent to 7 percent, leading to the presumption that police had previously been planting evidence to reach arrest quotas. The new courts have also issued arrest warrants that are a vital tool in suppressing gang and organized crimes. However, in spite of the success with the twenty-four-hour courts, Guatemala's judicial performance remains inadequate. Judges are often influenced by organized crime, political elite, and racial or ethnic affiliations. Costs to bring legal suit are too high. The national-level judiciary is not obliged to provide reasons for their decisions. The complexity and length of legal processes are also a problem, as is the limited investigative capacity of the public prosecutor's office, which results in very few indictments for corruption crimes. *Sources:* Transparency International, *National Integrity Study 2007* (Berlin: Transparency International, 2007); Global Integrity, *Global Integrity Report 2006: Guatemala*; USAID, "24-Hour Courts Rule of Law Program Fact Sheet," http://www.usaid.gov/gt/docs/fact_sheet_rol_24hour_courts.pdf (accessed November 2010).

Financial Management Program. The World Bank-sponsored Integrated Financial Management program sought to increase the effectiveness, efficiency, and transparency of public sector financial management and control. The project targeted consolidation of financial management systems in Guatemalan municipalities, supported improvements in human resources management, strengthened the Office of the Comptroller General, and supported the government's e-government agenda.

Results. The project produced significant results. The web-based Integrated Financial Management System is fully operational. Ten decentralized entities and seven large municipalities use the system. Over 318 municipalities operate transparent financial systems for local governments that have been made mandatory by the Controller General's Office. The e-procurement system has been implemented and serves as a highly effective tool to combat corruption and promote efficiency and effectiveness. *Source:* World Bank, "Status of Project Execution—FY07, Latin America and the Caribbean Region," 2007, http://www1.worldbank.org/operations/disclosure/SOPE/FY07/LAC-SOPE_FY07_FINAL.pdf (accessed November 2010).

Sierra Leone

Support of the Anticorruption Commission. An Anti-Corruption Commission was established in 2000 (sponsored by DFID, World Bank, GTZ, and UNDP) to investigate instances of alleged or suspected corruption. The commission was meant to take necessary measures to eradicate and suppress corrupt practices by investigating and prosecuting corrupt officials, publishing reports, and fostering public support in the fight against corruption.

Results. The commission failed to move on any high-level prosecutions. Due to low political will, there has been no engagement of other governance pillars or stakeholders to fight corruption. The commission has failed to report on corruption cases or conduct studies or investigations. As a result, donor organizations were advised to withdraw funding. *Source:* Joel Cutting and Gladwell Otieno, "Annual Review 2006 of DFID Support to Anticorruption Commission Phase 2 in Sierra Leone," Department for International Development, UK, January 25, 2007, http://www.dfid.gov.uk/pubs/files/anticorruption-sierraleone.pdf (accessed November 2010).

Private Sector Reform Program. The USAID-supported Peace Diamond Alliance (PDA) was launched to improve control and management of the diamond industry. The program aimed at eliminating money laundering, corruption, and unfair labor practices in the industry. The PDA worked with local and international alliance members to support transparent diamond management, develop competitive buying schemes, train miners, track diamonds, address corruption and child mining issues, and ensure that the diamond business sustains the welfare of Sierra Leonean citizens.

Results. NGO and government representatives, diamond sellers, and mine workers were trained in the efficient management of the diamond trade. Internationally recognized buyers and mining corporations helped to design new transparent business practices, as well as practices that protected miners from exploitation. As a result, legal export of diamonds increased from $1.5 million in 1999 to over $70 million in 2003, benefiting communities with substantial tax revenues to fund community needs of public structures, markets, and schools. Proceeds to mining communities reached $312,000 in 2002 and over $500,000 by the end of 2003. *Source:* USAID, "Peace Diamond Alliance Launched 2003," October 1, 2003, http://africastories.usaid.gov/search_details.cfm?storyID=210&countryID=22&sectorID=0&yearID=4 (accessed December 7, 2010). "Peace Diamond Alliance Helps Mining Communities in Sierra Leone," 2004, http://africastories.usaid.gov/search_details.cfm?storyID=210&countryID=22&sectorID=0&yearID=4 (accessed December 7, 2010).

Burundi

Judicial Reform Program. GTZ and the German Ministry of Justice supported the reconstruction of the judicial system in improving the efficiency, transparency, quality, and internal control of the legal system. The judiciary lacked financial resources, qualified staff, coordination, and legal documentation that would create public trust, awareness of rights, and public access. The program provided logistical and technical support to selected courts, and published a bimonthly legal journal to educate the public about existing laws, new laws, and the challenges of the Burundian legal system.

Results. Despite some reluctance, the courts have published some of their verdicts, making them more accountable for their decisions. A database has been created for all Supreme Court decisions. Four court buildings have been modernized and 240 *bashingantahe* (traditional legal authorities) and paralegals have been trained. The program has been relatively successful in training staff, building courts, and pushing for transparency, thus creating the framework for a more efficient and accountable system. However, it is acknowledged that more needs to be done to increase public access to the courts, overcome excessive appeals costs, and reduce lengthy judicial processes. *Sources:* Anti-Corruption Resource Center, "Support in Reconstructing the Judicial System of Burundi," http://www.u4.no/projects/project.cfm?id=682 (accessed December 7, 2010); Global Integrity, Global Integrity Report 2007: Burundi, http://report.globalintegrity.org/Burundi/2007 (accessed December 7, 2010).

Civil Society Program. USAID funded the Strengthen Civil Society project to empower CSOs and local communities to advocate for their rights. The project supported expanded radio broadcasting, civil society involvement in legislative drafting, expanded citizen-government dialogue, and citizen education programs. The project strengthened transitional institutions and the peace process by advocating for effective government, the rule of law, and conflict mitigation.

Results. Training was provided for 24 journalists and 723 radio programs were broadcasted on peace, elections, conflict, impunity, repatriation, refugees, the rights of women and children, and the role of UN forces. Communities in 11 provinces were trained to resolve their own conflicts and participated in local projects to rehabilitate community infrastructure, sports centers, schools, and potable water and electricity supplies. A radio series nurtured the seeds of conflict transformation by telling stories of courageous Burundians who saved lives across different ethnic groups. As a result of community mobilization, legal amendments have been adopted to combat sexual violence and protect women and children. *Sources:* USAID, Democracy and Governance Data Sheet, http://www.usaid.gov/policy/budget/cbj2006/afr/pdf/bi695-006.pdf (accessed December 7, 2010); see also USAID, "Burundi Annual Report FY 2005."

Papua New Guinea

Parliamentary Reform Program. UNDP support to the national parliament targeted increased effectiveness, transparency, and accountability for parliamentary members and provincial administrations through capacity building workshops and technical support. The program aimed to strengthen the legislative, oversight, and representative roles of parliamentarians by enhancing linkages between national and provincial parliaments and strengthening the parliamentary committee system.

Results. The project was deemed to be unsuccessful due to a lack of political will and coordination with the parliamentary secretariat and speaker. The continuing displacement of parliamentary staff created, lack of ownership of the program and produced misunderstandings of the project's objectives. *Source:* UNDP, "Papua New Guinea," http://www.undp.org.pg (accessed December 7, 2010).

Decentralization Program. The Governance and Implementation Fund (GIF) (2004–07) was supported by Australia and New Zealand as a postwar recovery mechanism for the formerly rebellious Bougainville province. The GIF implemented programs to strengthen public service delivery by involving civil society participation in decision making and planning, and included programs to develop the Bougainville constitution, judiciary reform, local infrastructure strengthening, decentralization projects related to planning, budgeting and revenue allocation, and provincial economic growth. The GIF was funded at approximately US$2.5 million per year.

Results. Through GIF efforts, Bougainville's constitution was finalized and planned elections were held for an autonomous government. Implementation of the Fiscal Responsibility Act in 2006 has improved fiscal management and accountability. Bougainville has increased its capacity for planning, human resource reform, and decentralization efforts. GIF activities to rebuild infrastructure and reform the cocoa industry has restored Bougainville's status as PNG's largest cocoa producer, supporting peaceful economic development and stability in the former conflict region. *Sources:* Regan, "External versus Internal Incentives in Peace Processes;" AusAID, "Australian Aid to Bougainville," June 2010, http://www.ausaid.gov.au/country/png/bougainville.cfm.

Media Program. AusAID's Media for Development Initiative worked closely with the Media Council and the National Broadcasting Corporation to increase the quality and operational strength of local media representatives, thus contributing to more accountable governance. Special attention was paid to strengthening rural radio networks.

Results. Media are actively involved in reporting on anticorruption initiatives and serve as the premier source of information about cases of corruption throughout the country. Even the government-owned media station reports on corruption cases. The Media Council has taken a leadership role in supporting community campaigns and training journalists. *Sources:* AusAID, "Papua New Guinea Annual Program Performance Update 2006–07," http://www.ausaid.gov.au/publications/pdf/png_appr_2007.pdf (accessed December 7, 2010).

Liberia

Governance Reform Program. USAID launched the Building Recovery and Reform through Democratic Governance (BRDG) initiative to increase the scope of Liberia's statebuilding efforts. BRDG provided technical assistance and grants to support planning, budgeting, communications, and coordination to help build state legitimacy. The program strengthened communication systems, empowered effective political responses to local problems, and supported regional activities to strengthen the Mano River Union.

Results. Independent Star Radio increased broadcasting to enhance civic and local budget and anticorruption awareness activities. The national judicial system was kept accountable by publicizing legislator and official attendance and performance reports (legislative report cards). BRDG also assisted the Ministry of Lands, Mines, and Energy in establishing ten regional offices to oversee the diamond industry and make it more accountable (part of the Kimberley Process Certification Scheme). The Mano River regional and local youth parliaments created a subregional network of young people that advocates for peace and human rights. *Source:* USAID Transition Initiatives, "USAID/OTI Liberia Field Report, April–June 2007," http://www.usaid.gov/our_work/cross-cutting_programs/transition_initiatives/country/liberia/rpt0607.html (accessed December 7, 2010).

Civil Society Program. USAID-sponsored support for West African civil society networks strengthened capacity building in civil society organizations for anticorruption and broadcasting initiatives. The project promoted wide usage of the Internet and community radio networks to mobilize democracy and anticorruption initiatives.

Results. In Liberia, CSOs are generally active in the policymaking process and participated in development of the Liberian Anticorruption Act.

Liberian CSOs formed a coalition to work on transparency in the extractive industries, as well as on anticorruption awareness campaigns. *Source:* West African Regional Program (WARP), "Data Sheet," 2005, http://www. usaid.gov/policy/budget/cbj2006/afr/pdf/warp624-007.pdf (accessed December 7, 2010).

Financial Management Program. The multidonor Governance and Economic Management Assistance Program (GEMAP) implemented good economic governance projects to enhance transparency and accountability of state institutions.

Results: Revenue collection at state-owned enterprises increased substantially in the first year after international financial controllers were introduced. Leakage of revenues has been reduced. The Ministry of Finance indicates that government revenue receipts have increased by 37 percent after the introduction of new streamlined procedures that also resulted in improved customer satisfaction. However, over the short term, customers of the state-owned enterprises still complained about poor levels of service and lack of accountability and transparency. *Source:* Dodd and Nelson, "USAID Activities under GEMAP in Liberia."

Index

About the Author

Bertram I. Spector, executive director at the Center for Negotiation Analysis and senior technical director at Management Systems International, has extensive experience conducting negotiation research and directing international development assistance programs in support of good governance, anticorruption, and civil society. Working with USAID, the World Bank, and other international organizations, he has advised governmental decision makers in the development and implementation of anticorruption strategies in Eastern Europe, the former Soviet Union, Africa, Asia, and Latin America. He was director of the Processes of International Negotiation (PIN) project at the International Institute for Applied Systems Analysis (Austria), where he conducted negotiation research and advised practicioners in the UN system. He is editor-in-chief of *International Negotiation: A Journal of Theory and Practice.*